Difficult Contexts
for Therapy

Ericksonian Monographs

Ericksonian Monographs   Number 10

Difficult Contexts
for Therapy

Edited by
Stephen R. Lankton, M.S.W.
Jeffrey K. Zeig, Ph.D.

BRUNNER/MAZEL Publishers • New York

We would like to express our special thanks for assistance with this monograph to:

Seyma Calihman, M.S.S.W.   Joseph Hicks, M.Ed.
Sally Franek, Ph.D.   Marian Richetta, M.A.
                    Hillel Zeitlin, L.C.S.W.

Library of Congress Cataloging-in-Publication Data

Difficult contexts for therapy / edited by Stephen R. Lankton, Jeffrey K. Zeig
     p. cm. — (Ericksonian monographs; no. 10)
    Includes bibliographical references.
    ISBN 0-87630-749-7
    1. Psychotherapy. 2. Erickson, Milton H. 3. Hynotism—Therapeutic use. 4. Psychotherapy—Case studies. I. Lankton, Stephen R. II. Zeig, Jeffrey K. III. Series.
    [DNLM: 1. Erickson, Milton H. 2. Hypnosis. 3. Psychotherapy. W1 ER44 no. 10 1995 / WM 415 D569 1995]
RC480.5.D525 1995
616.89'14—dc20
DNLM/DLC
for Library of Congress   94-5346
                                               CIP

Published by
BRUNNER/MAZEL, INC.
19 Union Square West
New York, New York 10003

Manufactured in the United States of America
10 9 8 7 6 5 4 3 2 1

Ericksonian Monographs

The *Ericksonian Monographs* publish only original manuscripts dealing with Ericksonian approaches to hypnosis, family therapy, and psychotherapy, including techniques, case studies, research, and theory.

The *Monographs* will publish only those articles of highest quality that foster the growth and development of the Ericksonian approach and exemplify an original contribution to the fields of physical and mental health. In keeping with the purpose of the *Monographs*, articles should be prepared so that they are readable by a heterogeneous audience of professionals in psychology, medicine, social work, dentistry, and related clinical fields.

Publication of the *Ericksonian Monographs* shall be on an irregular basis, no more than three times per year. The *Monographs* are a numbered, periodical publication. Dates of publication are determined by the quantity of high-quality articles accepted by the Editorial Board and the Board of Directors of the Milton H. Erickson Foundation, Inc., rather than by calendar dates.

Advice for Authors

Manuscripts should be *submitted in quintuplicate* (five copies) with a 100- to 150-word abstract to William J. Matthews, Ph.D., 22 Foxglove Lane, Amherst, MA 01002. Manuscripts of lengths varying from 15 to 100 typed double-spaced pages will be considered for publication. Submitted manuscripts cannot be returned to authors. Authors using electronic storage should also send a floppy disk containing the file. Call 413-253-2966 for any additional help.

Style and format of submitted manuscripts must adhere to the instructions described in the *Publication Manual of the American Psychological Association* (third edition, 1983). The manuscripts will be returned for revision if reference citations, preparation of tables and figures, manuscript format, avoidance of sexist language, copyright permission for cited material, title-page style, etc., do not conform to the *Manual*.

Copyright ownership must be transfered to the Milton H. Erickson Foundation, Inc., if your manuscript is accepted for publication. The Editor's acceptance letter will include a form explaining copyright release, ownership, and privileges.

Reference citations should be scrutinized with special care to credit originality and avoid plagiarism. Referenced material should be carefully checked by the author prior to the first submission of the manuscript.

Charts and photographs accompanying the manuscripts must be presented in camera-ready form.

Copy editing and galley proofs will be sent to the authors for revisions. Manuscripts must be submitted in clearly written, acceptable, scholarly English. Neither the Editor nor the Publisher is responsible for correcting errors of spelling and grammar: the manuscript, after acceptance, should be immediately ready for publication. Authors should understand that a charge will be passed on to them by the publisher for revision of galleys.

Prescreening and review procedures for articles are outlined below. Priority is given to those articles that conform to the designated theme for the upcoming *Monographs*. All manuscripts will be prescreened, without the author's name, by the Editor or one member of the Editorial Board and one member of either the Continuing Medical Education (CME) Committee or the Board of Directors of the Milton H. Erickson Foundation, Inc.

Final acceptance of all articles is at the discretion of the Board of Directors of the Milton H. Erickson Foundation, Inc. Their decisions will be made after acceptable prescreened articles have been reviewed and edited by a minimum of four persons: two Editorial Board members, one member of the CME committee or the Board of Directors, and the Editor. Occasionally, reviewers selected by the Editor will assist in compiling feedback to authors. The final copy of an accepted paper should be sent also on a floppy disk by authors using electronic storage.

Feedback for authors and manuscript revision will be handled by the Editor between one and two months after submission of the prepared manuscript. Additional inquiries are welcome if addressed to the Editor.

Contents

Contributors   ix

Introduction
by Stephen R. Lankton and Jeffrey K. Zeig   xi

Hypnosis and Cancer Pain: Ericksonian Approach
Versus Standardized Suggestibility Testing
by Hansjörg Ebell   1

Uncovering Resources in Patients in Medical Settings
by Ricardo Figueroa Quiroga   9

On the Social Nature of the Unconscious Mind: Pearson's
Brick, Wood's Break, and Greenleaf's Blow
by Eric Greenleaf   16

Managed Care, HMOs, and the Ericksonian Perspective
by Michael F. Hoyt   25

Ericksonian Approaches to Curiosity in the Treatment of
Incest and Sexual Abuse Survivors
by Paula J. Haymond   37

Personality Restructuring from an Ericksonian Perspective
by Don Malon and Wendy Hurley   50

Symbolic Therapy: Two Cases of Refusal to Attend School
by Keiichi Miyata   61

The Effects of Therapeutic Stories on Adolescent Behavior
Patterns
by Harry Vincenzi   69

How Ambiguous Are Ambiguous Tasks?
by Marc Franchot Weiss   82

The "February Man" Technique: Successful Replications
by Dawn M. White   102

Ericksonian Communication and Hypnotic Strategies in
the Management of Tics and Tourette Syndrome in Children
and Adolescents
by Daniel P. Kohen   117

Contributors

Hansjörg Ebell, M.D. private practice, Munich, Germany

Ricardo Figueroa Quiroga, M.Sc. Instituto Milton H. Erickson de Guadalajara, Guadalajara, Jalisco, Mexico

Eric Greenleaf, Ph.D. private practice, Berkeley, CA

Paula J. Haymond, Ed.D. private practice, Houston, TX

Michael F. Hoyt, Ph.D. Kaiser Permanente Medical Center, Department of Psychiatry, Hayward, CA

Wendy Hurley, M.A. private practice, Santa Cruz, CA

Daniel P. Kohen, M.D. Associate Professor, Departments of Pediatrics and Family Practice & Community Health, University of Minnesota, Minneapolis, MN

Don Malon, Ph.D. School of Social Service, St. Louis University, St. Louis, MO

Keiichi Miyata, M.A., Associate Professor, Faculty of Education, Niigata University, Niigata-Shi, Japan

Harry Vincenzi, Ed.D. private practice, Philadelphia, PA

Marc Franchot Weiss, Ph.D. Milton H. Erickson Institute of Northern Illinois, Chicago, IL

Dawn M. White, Ph.D. private practice, Cornville, AZ

Introduction

We are happy to provide this volume of the *Ericksonian Monographs*, containing 11 articles from internationally recognized experts on Ericksonian therapy. The first 10 articles are accepted papers from the Fifth International Erickson Congress, which was organized by The Milton H. Erickson Foundation and was held in December 1992 in Phoenix, Arizona. These collected papers pertain to difficult therapeutic contexts, some of which are examined as theoretical problems and others as they pertain to practice and research. They cover working with cancer pain, school avoidance, school classrooms, extramural assignments, HMOs, head injury recovery, and other difficult contexts. We will briefly introduce the individual contributions.

Problems in assessing hypnotizability are addressed by Hansjörg Ebell in his chapter, "Hypnosis and Cancer Pain: Ericksonian Approach Versus Standardized Suggestibility Testing." Ebell examined the comprehensive role of the treatment context in providing pain control training to cancer patients. He conducted a year-long pilot study on subjective response to suggestibility measures, contextual variables, and the interactional levels of the patients. This article describes that research and his findings that concentrating on measurable hypnotizability may mislead practicioners about hypnotic ability when intervening in the clinical setting.

Another difficult context for therapy is that in which the therapist finds subjects already unconscious! This is the problem addressed by Ricardo Figueroa Quiroga in "Uncovering Resources in Patients in Medical Settings." He presents two cases in which the therapist's persistence and open-mindedness lead to some eye-opening results. One case concerns recovery from unconsciousness, the other blood flow control. It is additionally interesting to see both Quiroga's reluctance and his successes in dealing with skepticism among colleagues.

"On the Social Nature of the Unconscious Mind: Pearson's Brick, Wood's Break, and Greenleaf's Blow" by Eric Greenleaf is a unique paper, providing insight into the healing process Greenleaf used to survive and overcome severe injury and trauma. As the title indicates, he accessed resources derived from stories he learned from Pearson and Wood, who spoke of their own healing and recovery. Greenleaf reflects on the possible role of hypnosis as the variable linking social networks and neurophysiology, and provides a glimpse of the phenomenological impact of hypnotic language in his recovery.

Michael Hoyt's pragmatic chapter, "Managed Care, HMOs, and the Ericksonian Perspective," describes variables important for treatment in managed health care settings, a topic of considerable interest in today's economic climate. He notes that many features of the Ericksonian approach are well suited to this context. After covering his reasons, which include the emphasis on specific problem solving, flexibility of time, accountability, and multiple formats for therapy, he provides case examples to demonstrate his hypotheses.

Paula J. Haymond focused on the therapeutic element of curiosity as central to change, especially in the treatment of incest and sexual abuse survivors. "Ericksonian Approaches to Curiosity in the Treatment of Incest and Sexual Abuse Survivors" provides two case examples that illustrate how adopting an attitude of curiosity toward an experience automatically reframes that experience and involves the client in creative problem solving.

"Personality Restructuring from an Ericksonian Perspective," as presented by Don Malon and Wendy Hurley, means reassociating and reorganizing the patient's phenomenal world. They illustrate how their therapy was influenced by Erickson in several important ways and how they have added emphasis on symbolic imagery and unconscious focus on feelings. The result of the latter is an approach to personality restructuring that progresses gradually and in many cases allows for integrated awareness.

Keiichi Miyata provides insight into his therapy work in Japan with "Symbolic Therapy: Two Cases of Refusal to Attend School" in which he presents two case studies using symbols in psychotherapy. One case involves a 15-session treatment of school and social avoidance in an adolescent boy, and the other a girl suffering from social isolation and rejection. Of special interest to this volume is the use of future-oriented and goal-directed interventions in a developmental framework as clients transform and modify their own "stories" about therapy.

Research in urban and low-income school settings is provided by Harry Vincenzi in "The Effects of Therapeutic Stories on Adolescent Behavior Patterns." Vincenzi studied 77 students with pretest and posttest scores on the Interpersonal Check List. The experimental group was provided weekly stories closely following the goal-oriented formats for metaphors by Lankton and Lankton. He traced both the teachers' and the students' reactions and found that this technique may be a very worthwhile aid to curriculum in this difficult context for therapy.

Marc Franchot Weiss answers an imposing question: What do jars, mountains, treats, and chops have in common? "How Ambiguous Are Ambiguous Tasks?" is a delightful and insightful contribution to the topic of these intriguing interventions. Weiss tells us how to use ambiguous tasks in the difficult context of extramural therapy. Many of his cases offer the same ambiguous assignment involving the alignment and study of three jars each evening. He thereby makes it possible to more clearly follow the impact of such assignments on the unique life of each client.

"The 'February Man' Technique: Successful Replications" by Dawn M. White is a succinct and useful summary of the interventions used in a recreation of Erickson's February Man intervention. She provides preliminary background and details the sessions prior to the intervention.

Daniel P. Kohen wrote "Ericksonian Communication and Hypnotic Strategies in the Management of Tics and Tourette Syndrome in Children and Adolescents" to describe his and his colleague's work with 35 youths with Tourette syndrome. This paper studies their nine years of work helping children construct self-regulatory actions in this difficult context by using an Ericksonian-inspired approach.

These are excellent papers that advance the seminal contributions of Milton Erickson. We are sure they will provide valuable insights for researchers, clinicians, and theorists.

Stephen R. Lankton, M.S.W.
Jeffrey K. Zeig, Ph.D.

Hypnosis and Cancer Pain: Ericksonian Approach Versus Standardized Suggestibility Testing

Hansjörg Ebell, M.D.

Pharmacological treatment based on WHO-guidelines is standard treatment for the symptomatic relief of cancer pain. Hypnosis can supplement reduction of pain and suffering by tapping individual coping resources. A topical overview of pertinent publications is augmented by the presentation of data concerning a controlled clinical study at Munich University Clinic. The relationship between an Ericksonian approach (audiotaped standardized induction, person to person instructions) and standardized suggestibility testing (Stanford Hypnotic Clinical Scale/Adults) will be discussed.

Approximately 50 percent of all patients who contact the Interdisciplinary Pain Unit of Munich University Clinic suffer from acute and chronic pain from the progression of cancer. They generally are treated with analgesics, including opiates. This procedure complies with the long-established guidelines of the World Health Organization.

In addition, psychosocial support measures have proven beneficial. The complexity of human pain requires treatment that targets not only physiological but also affective, cognitive, and behavioral components. In other words, a diversity of efforts must be undertaken both to reduce suffering and to minimize the disabling effects of disease and accompanying chemotherapy and surgery. Above all, the patient's own coping strategies and resources should be an integral part of any treatment program.

Hypnosis and self-hypnosis can serve the patient in his or her urgent need to control pain. (The specific effects of hypnosis in quasi-

Address correspondence to Hansjörg Ebell, M.D., Breisacherstr. 4, 81667 Munich, Germany.

1

experimental, clinical settings are detailed in, for example, Josephine Hilgard and Sam LeBaron's research [Hilgard & LeBaron, 1982] and, recently, in Karen Syrjala's report [Syrjala, Cummings, & Donaldson, 1992] on bone marrow transplant patients at Washington State University in Seattle. The controlled study of David Spiegel and his co-workers [Spiegel et al., 1989] provides another example.)

Case studies are commonly reported in the literature on hypnosis and pain control with cancer patients. Many authors (e.g., Barber & Gitelson, 1980; Erickson, 1959; Sacerdote, 1980) report surprising changes in pain perception, especially during terminal stages. At the First Congress on Hypnosis and Psychosomatic Medicine in Paris, in 1965, Milton Erickson (Erickson, 1967b) presented hypnosis techniques that he found effective for pain control (Table 1). To these techniques, Erickson adds:

> However, in all hypnotic procedures for the control of pain one bears in mind the greater feasibility and acceptability to the patient of indirect as compared with direct hypnotic suggestions and the need to approach the problem by indirect and permissive measures and by the employment of a combination of various of the methodological procedures described above. (1967b, p. 90)

A clinical researcher might proceed by selecting one or another of Erickson's strategies in order to test it on a patient. He might even ask the patient to make the choice. The researcher would then screen the patient for "suggestibility" using a valid and reliable scale (e.g., one of the Stanford scales). Perhaps, to ensure success, only those patients with high suggestibility scores would participate.

This procedure seems a fail-safe approach to meeting the demand for a controlled study by Turner and Chapman (1982) and Tan (1982). In any

---

Table 1

Application of Hypnosis for Pain Control

- Use of direct hypnotic suggestions for total abolition of pain
- Permissive indirect hypnotic abolition of pain
- Utilization of amnesia
- Employment of hypnotic analgesia
- Hypnotic anaesthesia
- Hypnotic replacement or substitution of sensations
- Hypnotic displacement of pain
- Hypnotic dissociation (time and body disorientation)
- Hypnotic reinterpretation of pain experience
- Hypnotic time distortion
- Offering hypnotic suggestions effecting a diminution of pain

---

From Erickson, 1967b.

case, this approach corresponds to the present-day hypotheses regarding "scientific" thinking at European university clinics.

A Personal Perspective

I would like to explain why I have subtitled this chapter "Ericksonian Approach *Versus* Standardized Suggestibility Testing." My primary post-graduate hypnosis training began with a traditional approach of offering direct and indirect suggestions. Then, when I began to work full time as an anesthesiologist in a pain clinic, I reread Erickson's (1966) famous story about the "tomato plant." It fascinated me that the desperate condition of a terminally ill cancer patient seemed to find successful resolution through the interspersing of suggestions. Erickson's case reports began to exert great influence on my approach to chronic pain patients.

I felt honored to be invited to present at a European hypnosis congress in 1985 (Ebell, 1985). I discussed my first few successful experiences with what I thought to be my "Ericksonian" approach. Professor Jean Lassner, chairman of this session, remarked dryly that, although he did find my stories interesting, I might have served scientific curiosity more effectively had I pointed out what did *not* work. (In retrospect, it embarrasses me somewhat to admit that it took me a couple of years of clinical experience to truly grasp the essence of his remark. In any case, it immediately made me stop bragging about being an "Ericksonian" therapist.)

David Cheek's work (Cheek, 1994; Cheek & LeCron, 1968; Rossi & Cheek, 1988) probably had the strongest influence on my way of working with pain patients. His ideomotor signaling approach, with or without formal trance induction, has become a valuable clinical tool. Most valuable, were the numerous shared experiences with the patients themselves; it was they who shaped my personal understanding of hypnosis. I noted entirely unexpected psychophysiological changes to evolve all by themselves out of spontaneous and/or induced trance states. I felt more and more convinced that the factors of human relationship, existential need, and motivation have a decisive and determining influence on which trance phenomena will arise and when. Of great importance, these effective trance phenomena often seemed to occur in their own way; they did not manifest themselves as my hypnotic suggestions had intended them to.

In his article on "Deep Hypnosis and Its Induction," Milton Erickson (1952) himself remarks:

The securing of comparable degrees of hypnosis in different subjects and similar trance states in the same subject at different times frequently constitutes a major problem.

The reasons for these difficulties derive from the fact that hypnosis depends upon inter- and intrapersonal relationships. Such relationships are inconstant and alter in accord with personality reactions to each hypnotic development. Additionally, each individual personality is unique, and its patterns of spontaneous and responsive behavior necessarily vary in relation to time, situation, purposes served, and the personalities involved....(p.7)

My own clinical experience corroborated Erickson's point. But this meant that in order to demonstrate to skeptical clinicians the effects of hypnosis for pain relief in a controlled study, I would have to pay attention to "inter- and intrapersonal relationships." Additionally, whatever measures I evolved, had to fit into the daily clinical routine. So, what approach could balance the high level of standardization necessary for scientific reasons on one hand, with the need to allow for the patient's individuality on the other?

Description and Testing of Treatment Concept

I developed the following "rationale" to examine the possible role of hypnosis in what I have come to call a "comprehensive" treatment concept for cancer-related pain: The treatment operates on three major operational treatment levels simultaneously: intrapersonal, interactional, and contextual. Although I must discuss them successively, no hierarchy is implied; in practice, any one level can present itself as a priority at any given time. Determined priorities are variable, personal, and situational.

Let us look at the *intrapersonal level* first:

Patients received audiotaped instructions for self-hypnosis. I did the recordings myself, and they contained standardized direct and indirect positive suggestions. These included:

— an eye fixation induction
— pacing of breathing, tension, and relaxation
— suggestions to find a place of rest, comfort, and well-being, and *there*, to imagine actively, with all senses, a personal activity
— following, a silence of several minutes, combined with an open-ended suggestion to use whatever came up as appropriate
— last, a posthypnotic suggestion for sleep and refreshed awakening or reorientation

My hypothesis was that actually listening to these instructions, perhaps even memorizing them, or modifying them personally, enabled the patient to induce rest and comfort. I made no direct suggestions that negated pain. I did not have to, because I understood that whatever hypnotic phenomena the patient would then develop would be the right ones for personally coping with pain. Furthermore, patients were encouraged to develop curiosity about the possibilities of self-hypnosis per se.

Second, the *interactional level*:

My role with the patient was that of a coach: I gave advice about the most effective way for that person to use the tape and—in order to minimize dependence—I encouraged any and all personal modification. The patient's development was monitored in weekly personal contacts with a team member. The current status was evaluated in team sessions.

The third, or *contextual level*:

All elements regarding the framework of the study happen on this level. The contextual level is the junction where the treatment coincides with the process of its evaluation.

Evaluating the study required using standard suggestibility testing, and the Stanford Hypnotic Clinical Scale for Adults was chosen. The scale was administered by a medical graduate student, who was introduced to the patients as a team member. The patient was informed that the results of this test would not influence our offer of self-hypnosis and moreover, that the test itself might be a help in making self-hypnosis effective for pain control. Those with therapeutic contact with a patient had no access to his or her Stanford scores until the end of the study, thus diminishing bias on the part of the team.

The effects of drug treatment were regarded as a baseline condition of the prospective study. The patients committed themselves to the study on a contextual level when they agreed to self-hypnosis as an additional treatment measure, and to the randomization plan of the study design. They signed informed consent forms and were obliged to keep a daily "pain diary" for a minimum period of 10 weeks.

The pain diaries were evaluated with the help of analog scales that presented visually the amount of continuous pain, breakthrough pain attacks, suffering from pain, well-being, coping expectation, and experienced self-control. The use of analgesics and the number and character of self-hypnosis exercises also were evaluated.

Major outcome variables for statistical analysis were pain intensity (the sum of "continuous pain" and "breakthrough pain attacks"), suffering from pain, well-being, anxiety (measured by the State Trait Anxiety Index [STAI]); and use of analgesics (according to the stepladder of the World Health Organization guidelines).

We established these parameters in a one-year pilot study, after receiving a grant from the German Cancer Society (Deutsche Krebshilfe) in 1988. Afterward we carried out a two-treatment crossover study over a period of 15 consecutive months. Of the 342 cancer patients referred to our unit, all were eligible for the study. Sixty-one were interested in learning self-hypnosis for pain control and signed on. Only 32 patients, however, met all of the study's requirements.

Because the framework of this presentation does not allow for a comprehensive description of the complex crossover design, I shall report on an auxiliary exploratory data analysis that we conducted: We compared the baseline period and the first 4 weeks of treatment as if we had used a simple parallel-study design with two treatments: with and without self-hypnosis. Findings are presented in Table 2.

For major outcome variables, the visual analog scales measuring pain intensity and suffering from pain differed significantly between the two groups. The group that undertook self-hypnosis in addition to pharmacological treatment fared better than the group treated only pharmacologically. Well-being, STAI scores, and use of analgesics did not differ.

Before we had the results of statistical analyses of patients' scoring on the Stanford scale, all our study patients were classified as responsive or unresponsive to self-hypnosis. We arrived at these conclusions in intensive team workups, under the guidance of two supervisors experienced in the field of clinical hypnosis.

These sessions led to the following classification:

— Eleven patients reported the achievement of pain control.
— Twelve other patients reported the benefits of rest, relaxation and sleep. (Only 7 of the 12 who reported these beneficial effects personally modified the taped inductions.)
— A final group of 9 patients reported neither improved pain control nor any other benefits. This group was composed of patients with complicated intrapersonal and contextual conditions, such as marital difficulties.

In sum, 16 patients were considered "responsive" and 14 patients "unresponsive" to self-hypnosis. On the basis of these clinical estimates, we

Table 2
Treatment Findings with Self-Hypnosis in Comparison to Findings
Without Self-Hypnosis

Reduction in:
    pain intensity   0.0114*
    suffering   0.0164*
    (measured by "visual analog scales")

*Statistically significant ($p \leq .05$).

Table 3
Suggestibility (SHCS/A) and Clinical Effect of Self-Hypnosis

SHCS/A	Clinical Evaluation	
Score	Responsive	Unresponsive
5	3	—
4	3	2
3	4	3
2	6	5
1	—	2
0	—	1
Test refused	—	1
Total Patients (n = 32[a])	16	14

[a]For organizational reasons testing of two patients was not carried out.
SHCS/A = Stanford Hypnotic Clinical Scale/Adults.

correlated the occurrence of beneficial effects through self-hypnosis with the Stanford scores.

As indicated in Table 3, the Stanford scale score corroborates the clinical team's evaluation for 6 patients: the 3 patients scoring highest ("5") and the 3 patients scoring lowest. One patient rejected the test procedure, and two tests were not carried out for organizational reasons. The Stanford scale scores of the remaining 23 patients were of no predictive value in determining the clinical effect of self-hypnosis. Were we to have based our selection of patients susceptible to self-hypnosis on the Stanford scoring results, our choice would indeed, in retrospect, have been questionable.

In a clinical context, concentrating on measurable "hypnotizability" may mislead the practitioner who is attempting to judge the hypnotic abilities of patients.

From this perspective, the subtitle of this paper would have to be changed. Instead of presenting the issue as "Ericksonian Approach *versus* Standardized Suggestibility Testing," we are encountering the disparity that arises between the realities of treatment prerogatives and the problematic search for scientific proof.

References

Barber, J., & Gitelson, J. (1980). Cancer pain: Psychological management using hypnosis. *CA-A Cancer Journal for Clinicians, 30*, 3, 130–136.
Cheek, D. B. (1994). *Hypnosis: The application of ideomotor techniques.* Boston: Allyn and Bacon.
Cheek, D. B., & LeCron, L. M. (1968). *Clinical hypnotherapy.* New York: Grune &

Stratton.

Ebell, H. (1985). Hypnosis: Therapeutic hope for chronic pain patients? *Proceedings of the Fifth Central European Congress of Medical and Experimental Hypnosis* Unpublished (handout for congress participants).

Erickson, M. H. (1959). Hypnosis in painful terminal illness. *American Journal of Clinical Hypnosis, 1,* 117–121.

Erickson, M. H. (1966). The interspersal hypnotic technique for symptom correction and pain control. *American Journal of Clinical Hypnosis, 8,* 3, 198–209.

Erickson, M. H. (1967a). Deep hypnosis and its induction. In J. Haley (Ed.), *Advanced techniques of hypnosis and therapy* (p. 7). New York: Grune & Stratton.

Erickson, M. H. (1967b). An introduction to the study and application of hypnosis for pain control. In J. Lassner (Ed.) *Hypnosis and psychosomatic medicine* (pp. 83–92). New York: Springer.

Hilgard, J. R., & LeBaron, S. (1982). Relief of anxiety and pain in children and adolescents with cancer: Quantitative measures and clinical observations. *International Journal of Clinical and Experimental Hypnosis, 30,* 4, 417–442.

Rossi, E. L., & Cheek, D. B. (1988). *Mind-body therapy: Ideodynamic healing in hypnosis.* New York: Norton & Company.

Sacerdote, P. (1980). Hypnosis in terminal illness. In G. D. Burrows & L. Dennerstein (Eds.), *Handbook of hypnosis and psychosomatic medicine* (pp. 421–442). Amsterdam: Elsevier.

Spiegel, D., Kraemer, H. C., Bloom, J. R., & Gottheil, E. (1989). Effect of psychosocial treatment on survival of patients with metastatic breast cancer. *Lancet,* October 14, 888–891.

Syrjala, K. L., Cummings, C., & Donaldson, G. W. (1992). Hypnosis or cognitive behavioral training for the reduction of pain and nausea during cancer treatment: A controlled clinical trial. *Pain, 48,* 137–146.

Tan, S. (1982). Cognitive and cognitive-behavioral methods for pain control: A selective review. *Pain, 12,* 201–228.

Turner, J. A., & Chapman, C. R. (1982). Psychological interventions for chronic pain: A critical review. *Pain, 12,* 23–46.

Uncovering Resources in Patients in Medical Settings

Ricardo Figueroa Quiroga, M.Sc.

The author presents two different procedures to elicit responses from patients who may not be fully conscious at the moment of the intervention. The first case pertains to a woman with depression who was hospitalized for the second time in one year, and who was in a stuporous and semicatatonic state for six days. She was helped to emerge from her state by having her name called while her breathing rhythm was paced. The second case involves a procedure used with patients under general anesthesia to stop bleeding during surgery of the tonsils or nose.

The use of Ericksonian approaches to hypnosis implies the acceptance of certain basic principles. Milton H. Erickson had many definitions of hypnosis, several of which are contained in his works. I have used some of them as a theoretical background to guide my practice. For example, Erickson (1959, 1985b) defined hypnosis "as a state of special awareness characterized by a receptiveness to ideas" (p. 223). Erickson presented many ideas to his patients to provide a wide range from which they could choose. He noted that the process of using hypnosis is "a matter of getting the patient to be receptive to ideas, and to respond to ideas" (p. 148). The Ericksonian therapist must be skilled in numerous ways of presenting ideas to the patient, because, "Hypnosis doesn't come from mere repetition. It comes from getting your patient to accept an idea and to respond to that idea" (Erickson, 1958/1985a, p. 143). The patient has to respond to the ideas presented to him, and in that moment the real magic begins. The therapist has to respond to the patient and to start building the intervention, tailoring it to fit the patient (J. Zeig, personal communication, 1990). In customary therapy, the patient in early sessions describes the present-

Address correspondence to Ricardo Figueroa Quiroga, M.Sc., Instituto Milton H. Erickson de Guadalajara, Progreso #271, P. B., Guadalajara, Jalisco 44150, Mexico.

9

ing problem. The therapist makes a diagnosis according to the theoretical lenses she is using, and plans the therapy, adjusting to the patient's needs.

An implied principle may be presented as a question: Is consciousness necessary to develop a hypnotic trance? The common answer is "Definitely yes!" Erickson (1958/1980b) stated that "the primary purpose served in the experimental and clinical use of hypnosis is the communication of ideas and understandings for the purpose of eliciting responsive behavior at both psychological and physiological levels" (p. 192). The basic tenet is: First get a response! If the patient is in a state of full consciousness, then it is relatively easy to secure a response; but if the patient is not—is, for example, stuporous—how does one get a response? How do you hypnotize a patient who is not fully conscious?

Case One

I was requested by a psychiatrist to hypnotize one of his patients, who was suffering from depression. The woman was 42 years old and in the process of divorcing, and her husband was withholding money, had taken the car, had tried to get her out of the house, and was doing his best to convince their sons to blame the divorce on her. The woman had a low educational level (ninth grade), and she was unable to make a living because she lacked marketable skills. Her parents provided some money for living expenses, and pressured her to stop the divorce proceedings. She had become depressed, was hospitalized a first time, received electroconvulsive therapy (ECT) and medication, and was discharged two weeks later. After three months she was back in the hospital. The psychiatrist explained to me that he did not want to use ECT again because of the patient's heart problem. The patient was, in his words, "very hysterical." He added that she would be a good subject for hypnosis, and suggested that I hypnotize her in an attempt to alleviate her depression.

When I arrived at the hospital I was received by a psychiatric resident and directed to the ward. On the way, the resident expressed great interest in hypnosis and requested to be present. After I explained to him that the patient would have to give her consent, he described the patient's condition: she had been in the hospital for 20 days. She came in walking but had "deteriorated very fast," and now she was bedridden. There was a problem with blood flow to her legs, because of a lack of mobility, and she was "semi-catatonic" from the waist up. When we arrived at the woman's bedside, her eyes were rolled up so that only the sclera was visible. Another resident and a nurse were trying to insert an intravenous catheter into a vein in her right foot. During five attempts to insert the needle, the woman exhibited no reaction. To complete the picture, three more psychiatic residents appeared at the door asking when the hypnosis was going to start.

The first resident told me he would "wake up" the patient in a moment. He put his hand on her back and raised her to a sitting position. Her head was upright, her arms stiff and extended. Her eyes remained fixed. The resident slapped her several times on the face as he yelled to her to wake up. Nothing happened. He lowered her back to a supine position and said, "She is all yours. Hypnotize her."

I mentally reviewed all my favorite quotations from Milton Erickson, and not one seemed usable. The impulse to leave was very strong—but the "wise guy" smiles of the psychiatric residents were extremely offensive. I decided that the patient was not conscious but her unconscious mind was potentially accessible, so long as her hearing was not affected. I recalled reading about the recovery of memories from anesthetized patients; they could register meaningful sounds and words spoken in the surgical room (Cheek, 1981). I also remembered that an individual's name, ingrained since birth, is rarely forgotten; and I recalled the maxim "First you have to get the patient to respond."

I sat down, observed the breathing of the patient, and started to call her name (Carmen), my timing pacing her breathing rhythm—"Car" as she inhaled and "men" while she exhaled. After 15 minutes the residents left. I continued for 3 hours and 45 minutes, by which time the only visible response had been several eyelid closures.

When I arrived at the hospital the next afternoon, Carmen was in another room with her legs raised higher than her head. Heaters were directed toward her legs. The resident explained that there was concern that circulatory problems could develop. I repeated the procedure I had performed on the previous day and added gentle pressure on Carmen's right hand (which was on top of the blanket) when she inhaled. I released at the moment she exhaled. After approximately 90 minutes, Carmen made a very slight response with her hand. I continued the procedure. Soon Carmen was responding with more pressure with her hand. Then, after a bare suggestion of an upward movement, her hand started to rise. I started a hide-and-seek pattern with her hand: Carmen would seek for my hand, grab it, and release it. I gave a little pull on her arm, and it rose from the bed, remaining in the air.

I said, "Close your eyes, relax very deeply, and fall asleep." Carmen closed her eyes. Her body relaxed, her arm remaining suspended in the air. Later, I offered a wide series of suggestions concerning walking in the woods, being at the sea shore and enjoying life. The next step was to give straightforward and direct suggestions about the next-day visit by her

personal physician: She was to wake up, sit on the bed, talk with the doctor, feel very hungry, request food, rise and start walking a bit, and, in
general, feel better. She had no need to recall anything about me, except if
her unconscious mind decided it would be useful. The patient was instructed to sleep soundly all night; she would awaken fresh and energetic
the next morning. The instructions for the physician were recorded in her
chart. The next morning she did as had been directed, made a good recovery, and was discharged from the hospital eight days later.

Case Two

During a lecture at a state-owned general hospital, an otolaryngologist
surgeon requested information about the possibility of using hypnosis to
stop or reduce bleeding during surgery, especially tonsil and nose surgery,
which she performed almost daily. The common procedures were time-
consuming and delayed surgery on other patients.

In my answer, I referred to the professional literature, which provided
me with the basis for an impromptu procedure: First I referred to the work
of Banks (1985) regarding the control of bleeding in the angiography suite,
in which the "patient is addressed as if he were obviously in trance" (Cheek,
1962c, p. 78). The suggestions used were as follows: "Excuse me, Mr. . . . ,
but you are leaking a little blood around the catheter where it goes into the
artery, and it really does make things a little more difficult for us. If you
would just stop the bleeding, it would be a big help."

The surgeons, hearing my response, replied that their patients were given
gas anesthesia and could not possibly respond in that state. I told them
about Cheek's statement (1981, p. 87) that "the unconscious mind main-
tains a channel of communication to the external world through the hearing sense at all times." Cheek published numerous reports on the subject
of recalling meaningful sounds under general anesthesia (Cheek, 1960,
1962a, 1962b, 1964) and authored an excellent literature review on the subject (Cheek, 1981). His studies determined that patients hear meaningful
sounds if the person speaking is someone significant to them, and there is
previously established rapport with the surgeon and/or the anesthetist.
Furthermore, the literature on clinical applications of hypnosis has many
references to bleeding control (Abramson, 1970; Dubin & Shapiro, 1974;
Lucas, Carroll, Finkelman, & Tocantins, 1962; Kroger & DeLee, 1957).

I next described the work of Dohan, Taylor, and Moss (1960), in which a
surgeon's answer to a patient's questions about length of hospital stay
and duration of convalescence showed a .80 positive correlation with actual patient performance. Therefore, if the surgeon gives information to

the patient about how she or he will respond, it is possible that the patient will respond in the expected direction. The surgeon might therefore talk casually to the patient outside of the surgical theater and provide positive expectations about subsequent patient bleeding behavior.

The final procedure I evolved was as follows: (a) The surgeon will talk with the patient outside of the surgical theater in a matter-of-fact way saying, "Mr./Ms.————, during surgery when I address you, I will do so by your first name, and you will know that I am talking to you. You may have some very small bleeding points, and I will request you to stop bleeding, and I expect you to do so." (b) If the patient answers that she or he does not know how to do this, the surgeon will reply, "Now, you have done it all your life—you just haven't noticed it." And then the surgeon will provide several examples from childhood, or of common accidents, such as small cuts from paper, staples, or knives, and nose bleeding, knee and elbow scratches, and will point out that all the bleeding stopped. (The time needed to stop the bleeding is not mentioned.) (c) During surgery, if there are bleeding points, the surgeon will ask the patient to stop bleeding.

Several of the surgeons present at the lecture expressed their doubts about the efficacy of the procedure. The surgeon who proposed the question offered to try it. With some reluctance, the surgeon used it initially with a nine-year-old boy, and the bleeding stopped in less than one minute. From then on, the procedure was repeated with the addition of suggestions of comfort, minimal pain, and good recovery after awakening from the anesthesia. The method has been used in more than 450 surgical procedures, with patients of all ages and both sexes, with positive results. Postoperative recovery has been fast, with few complaints of pain and few requests for analgesics. On 17 occasions there were no positive results; no explanation could be found for these instances.

Conclusion

It can be helpful to reevaluate the concept of "unconsciousness." Many people hold an ingrained belief that if a person is "unconscious," the *mind* is not functioning: If one is under the influence of chemical anesthesia or has received physical trauma and is not responding with one's conscious mind, then there is nothing anyone can do to contact or interact with that mind.

Two students who are friends of mine, Ana Rocio Gaspar and Juan Pablo Mudeci, worked for 3 months, 5 times a week, 2 hours each session, "pacing" an autistic child, and got responses from him: He touched them, moved to them, laughed, and made sounds. These behaviors were clearly directed to them and occurred in response to them. (Unfortunately the treatment was discontinued by the family because they didn't "like the changes in the child.")

In the case of Carmen, the process was similar: pacing, obtaining a response, developing the response, recovering "conscious functioning," developing a trance, doing therapy, and ending the trance. The problem was defined as "How do I make contact?" and my response was to use, in combination, two deeply ingrained elements: breathing and her first name.

In regard to the second case: It is common knowledge that in hypnosis, many subjects can control bleeding (Clawson & Sevade, 1975). The work by Banks (1985) clearly implies that it also is possible to develop bleeding control in the conscious state. There is much literature on the subject. The important element is, bleeding control may occur also with the patient under chemical anesthesia. Cheek (1981) clearly presents evidence of unconscious awareness during surgery—enough awareness to remember things that were said in the operating room.

My personal idea is that the anxiety state prior to surgery and the expectation of bleeding control expressed by the surgeon, along with the idea of "small" bleeding points, were responsible for the response by patients in Case Two. It seems clear that patients will accept any information that may help them reduce the uncertainty and anxiety engendered by the surgery. And it is better if that information elicits active participation instead of passivity. Therefore, if we have a "different" state of consciousness when we are "unconscious," the main problem is to develop a procedure to make use of it.

There is a relevant quotation from Erickson that I particularly like: "The point is, we ought to expect to find solutions rather than passively accepting a decree of 'uncurable.' Such an attitude of expectancy is far more conducive to our task of exploration, discovery and healing" (1958/1980a, p. 202).

References

Abramson, M. (1970, October). Self-hypnosis for hemophiliacs. Paper presented at the American Society of Clinical Hypnosis Workshop, University of Minnesota.

Bank, W. (1985). Hypnotic suggestion for the control of bleeding in the angiography suite. In S. Lankton (Ed.), *Ericksonian monographs, No. 1: Elements and dimensions of an Ericksonian approach* (pp. 76–88). New York: Brunner/Mazel.

Cheek, D. (1960). What does the surgically anesthetized patient hear? *Rocky Mountain Medical Journal, 57 (1)*, 49–53.

Cheek, D. (1962a). Areas of research into psychosomatic aspects of surgical tragedies now open through use of hypnosis and ideomotor questioning. *Western Journal of Surgery, Obstetrics and Gynecology, 70*, 137–142.

Cheek, D. (1962b). Emotions and purpura [Editorial]. *Journal of the American Medical Association, 1981,* 720–721.

Cheek, D. (1962c). Importance of recognizing that surgical patients behave as though hypnotized. *American Journal of Clinical Hypnosis, 4,* 227–238.

Cheek, D. (1964). Further evidence of persistence of hearing under chemo-anesthesia: Detailed case report. American Journal of Clinical Hypnosis, (1), 55–59.

Cheek, D. (1981). Awareness of meaningful sounds under general anesthesia: Considerations and a review of the literature 1959–1979. In H. Wain (Ed.), *Theoretical and clinical aspects of hypnosis* (p. 87). Miami: Miami Symposia Specialists.

Clawson, T. A. & Sevade, R. H. (1975). The hypnotic control of blood flow and pain. *American Journal of Clinical Hypnosis, 17,* 160–169.

Dohan, F., Taylor, E., & Moss, N. (1960). The role of the surgeon in the prolongation of uncomplicated surgical convalescence. *Surgery, Gynecology and Obstetrics, 111* (1), 49–57.

Dubin, L. & Shapiro, S. (1974). Use of hypnosis to facilitate dental extraction and hemostasis in a classic hemophiliac with high antibody titer to factor VIII. *American Journal of Clinical Hypnosis, 17,* 79–83.

Erickson, M. (1980a). A clinical experimental approach to psychogenic infertility. In E. Rossi (Ed.), *The collected papers of Milton H. Erickson on Hypnosis: Vol. 11. Hypnotic alteration of sensory, perceptual and psychophysical processes* (pp. 196–202). New York: Irvington.

Erickson, M. (1980b). The hypnotic alteration of blood flow: An experiment comparing waking and hypnotic responsiveness. In E. Rossi (Ed.), *The collected papers of Milton H. Erickson on Hypnosis: Vol. 11. Hypnotic alteration of sensory, perceptual and psychophysical processes* (pp. 192–195). New York: Irvington.

Erickson, M. (1985a). Reframing problems into constructive activity. In E. Rossi & M. Ryan (Eds.), *The seminars, workshops, and lectures of Milton H. Erickson* (Vol. 2, pp. 133–188). New York: Irvington.

Erickson, M. (1985b). Special states of awareness and receptivity. In E. Rossi & M. Ryan (Eds.), *The seminars, workshops, and lectures of Milton H. Erickson* (Vol. 2, pp. 223–242). New York: Irvington.

Kroger, W., & DeLee, S. (1957). Use of hypnoanesthesia for caesarean section and hysterectomy. *Journal of the American Medical Association, 163,* 442–444.

Lucas, O. N., Carroll, R. T., Finkelman, A., & Tocantins, L. M. (1962). Tooth extraction in hemophilia: Control of bleeding without use of blood, plasma, or plasma fractions. *Thrombosis et Diathesis Hemorrhagica, 8,* 209–220.

On the Social Nature of the Unconscious Mind: Pearson's Brick, Wood's Break, and Greenleaf's Blow

Eric Greenleaf, Ph.D.

The author's recovery from concussion and trauma after being struck by a speeding car was aided by stories he had been told 20 years earlier. Robert Pearson, M.D., and Don Wood both survived trauma to the head. Their stories unconsciously influenced the author in his survival and led to these remarks on the relational and social nature of the concept "unconscious mind."

Accident

One Friday morning, seven years ago, while walking across the street near my office, I was struck by a car moving at 45 miles per hour. The car arrived so suddenly that I did not see it approach, but *heard* it strike me. The force of the blow below my knee drove my body up over the hood and my forehead into the windshield. I saw a bright flash of light and was carried and thrown unconscious some 40 feet away.

When I regained consciousness I was lying on a traffic island, looking up into a circle of anxious faces: firemen, paramedics, bystanders. My head was cradled by a young woman sitting on the ground behind me. I heard her calmly say, "Just lie still. You're going to be all right." Immediately I had three thoughts, infused with the strongest possible emotion:

I love life and I want to live.

I'm going to tell everyone around me what I think and feel.

I'm going to get well as soon as I possibly can.

Address correspondence to Eric Greenleaf, Ph.D., 925 The Alameda, Berkeley, CA 94707

These three intentions guided me during my recovery, although I never consciously thought of them again. I began to speak to the paramedics and the young woman, explaining that I was angry at being hit, frightened, and sad that I was hurt. I wept and raged and joked. I asked each person's name (promptly forgetting it). I asked for my bag and I asked to be taken to Kaiser Hospital. Meanwhile, paramedics cut my clothes off, inserted IV needles, and started oxygen through a nasal cannula. I drifted in and out of consciousness.

At the hospital I was treated by several residents and nurses, who bathed my wounds and stitched my scalp. They asked me where I was from and I replied, "Brooklyn" (my childhood home). Each of them decided she or he was from Brooklyn too, and we had a lively conversation. Then I was taken to several examination rooms for x-rays and other tests. In between, left to myself in a busy urban emergency room, I spoke with any patient in proximity and exercised my swollen, edematous, cramped legs by walking and stretching as I talked.

The accident happened at 7:30 A.M. By 3:30 P.M. I was eager to go home. I asked the nurse, who asked the doctor. They agreed I could be released. I then asked the nurse to phone my wife to come for me, but she was unable to reach her. I asked the nurse to call a cab, which she did. The nurse gave me a large paper bag containing my unscarred shoes (they had flown off on impact) and my shredded, bloodstained clothes. She advised me to have my wife wake me every 2 hours during the night to establish my consciousness.

Wearing a hospital gown and foam shoes, I left the hospital and entered the taxi. The driver looked me over and said, "What happened to you?" I told him. "You're lucky!" he said. "I'm lucky I'm alive, but I'm unlucky the car hit me," I said.

I arrived home to find the house empty, my keys still in the missing bag I had taken with me that morning. I took a ladder from the yard, climbed in a window, found the bed, and went to sleep. Later, my wife arrived home. She had been frantically searching for me, having been told that I had had an accident. The emergency room had no record of my admission, so her calls to hospitals were fruitless. I rested and slept deeply most of the weekend. Monday morning I returned to work a regular week in my practice of psychotherapy and hypnotherapy, as I have for 20 years.

Recovery

Sometime during that first week I asked my wife to drive me through the scene of the accident at slow and fast speeds. I wanted to see the street as the car's driver had that early Friday morning. Back at work, I walked the path I had taken as always, crossing the 15-foot crosswalk where I had been struck. I crossed this street several times each day. For several months, while my legs recovered, I carried a stout cane for support, and took pleasure in brandishing it menacingly at drivers who came too close to me or honked impatiently as I slowly navigated the crossings. When I walked with my wife and son, each took one arm and reminded me to remain alert and careful.

Flashbacks of the accident began to arrive soon, frequent and unannounced. I would hear the clang of my body striking metal, see the hood of the car and the bright light above my left temple as my head struck the windshield. I have worked with several victims of trauma, and employed various hypnotherapeutic strategies to help them with flashbacks. But I found myself inclined to only watch the flashback each time it arrived. Hundreds of flashbacks, and several months later, the flashbacks visited less often, then rarely; finally, they stopped.

Neighbors, friends, and relatives visited—some eager, some concerned. I remember their feelings of care. I remember, too, one particular conversation. A sour, inquisitive neighbor lady came by each day to inquire about my health. She asked how I was doing. "I'm getting better," I said. "Oh," she responded, "sometimes you get better, then there are relapses." I slowly, and with great determination said, "Sometimes people have relapses, but I'm going to continue getting better."

And I did. The doctors could discover no brain damage (although I lost words from the "tip of my tongue" for several seconds during speech and thought for much of the following year) and no "permanent physical damage" (although my right knee remains weaker than my left). Their amazed looks and sucked-in breath when they considered the accident and compared its force with my body's "rude good health" gave me a great deal of pleasure. The positive medical reports also pleased the driver of the car that struck me, and his insurers. They settled a small sum on me in recompense for damages suffered. I took the money and traveled to Bali, where I had immense enjoyment filming masked trance dances and trance mediums at work with their patients.

Thinking like a Hypnotist

Few readers of this essay will know me personally, and those who do know me may not recognize me in this portrait of easy decisiveness and good judgment. Like all of us, I've stumbled as often as I've been bumped, and wavered and backtracked often enough. Yet in dealing with and recovering from this accident, in living through it, I automatically acted toward myself as I would have done toward a patient of mine—that is, I felt positive, respectful, and expectant. I had a genuine curiosity to see what would happen next. And as well, I held general goals for myself easily in the back of my mind:

I love life and I want to live.

I'm going to tell everyone around me what I think and feel.

I'm going to get well as soon as I possibly can.

The suddenness and surprise with which I was thrown into my predicament by a speeding car also seems to have thrown me into a state of great immediacy and responsiveness to both these previously unconscious goals and to the literal directions embodied in interactions between people. So, although I was physically quite helpless, I was, from the point of impact through my recovery from injury, determinedly active emotionally and interpersonally. When the kind young woman who cradled my head said, "Just lie still. You're going to be all right," I did, and I was. And when my nosy neighbor attempted to induce doubt in my recovery, I found myself crafting a counter-induction to sustain my progress.

I think that the active, immediate, and determined pursuit of my goals after being injured was coupled with a stance toward myself that was positive, curious, loving, and attentive to the literal nature of directives: the hypnotist's stance toward his patient. In following the advice we often give to patients to "take what is useful to you in meeting your goals in your own way and in your own good time, and leave the rest behind," I continue to wear the shoes I wore that day, which were ripped off my feet, unscuffed, by the force of the impact. The bag of clothes was quickly thrown away. Thank you, Dr. Erickson, for the words I have employed so often in my work.

Pearson's Brick, Wood's Break, Greenleaf's Blow

The thought came to me, "Oh, if Milton was only here!" The very next thought was "Well, buddy-boy, he *isn't* here, so you had better do it yourself."

—Robert Pearson, M.D.

Thinking about the ground from which my spontaneous reactions to trauma and recovery had sprung has led me back to the stories of the experiences of two men: Dr. Erickson's friend Robert Pearson, M.D., and my friend Don Wood. When I remembered their stories, I felt that they had prepared my unconscious mind for the actions I took more than 20 years later, during my own experience of trauma.

Pearson (1966) reported in "Communication and Motivation" his experience after being struck in the head by a 5-pound brick tossed from a roof 34 feet above him. He, like me, was struck by surprise so sudden and complete that his first sensation was of "an extremely loud noise." He struggled to retain consciousness and began to instruct those around him in providing proper care, transportation to the hospital, and medical treatment on his arrival. His realization that he had to "do it yourself" eventuated in a spontaneous analgesia for the extreme pain he felt. In hospital he "took charge again" of the treatment of his skull fracture, remaining alert to the conversations of the surgeon and anesthesiologist while anesthetized, even speeding his discharge:

> I said, "I have to go to San Francisco next Sunday. Under no circumstances will I sign myself out against your advice, but I do want to be discharged tomorrow. I'll make a deal with you: When you make rounds tomorrow, if you can find anything wrong on physical examination, I have any fever, I need anything for pain, my white count is elevated, or anything else is abnormal, I will stay in the hospital for as long as you say; otherwise you will discharge me."

Pearson won the bet. The doctor could find nothing abnormal on examination and discharged him. Pearson provides a charming example of his spontaneous emotional expressiveness during this brief hospital stay:

> My wife and a nurse were in the room, and my wife asked me how I felt. I replied, "Like I've been hit in the head by a goddamn brick!" The nurse interpreted this remark to mean that I was in severe pain, and gave me an injection. I asked her what she had given me, and she of course replied, "Why don't you ask your doctor?" I could have choked her with great pleasure.

Unable to command medical knowledge or to instruct the surgeon and nurses who treated my injuries, I likewise felt impelled to command what decisions I could. I insisted on being taken to the Kaiser hospital rather than to the emergency room preferred by the paramedics. I used my skills in relating to remain as conscious as I could and to have some say in my treatment and discharge. And I was most expressive of anger, sadness, and humor to those around me; I did not stand on ceremony.

Don Wood was a vigorous, athletic young man: a lumberjack one summer, medical orderly the next, psychology student during the school year. When I met him he was confined to a wheelchair with paraplegia. He told me that he had been riding on a bus going north for a graduate school interview when the bus was forced to swerve by a truck gone out of control. The bus went over a cliff, Don was thrown from the window, and the bus landed on him and broke his neck.

He told me that he spontaneously dissociated, so that he no longer felt his painful body, then calmly directed the rescue workers in the proper manner of handling a patient whose neck was broken. Don told me that during his recovery in the hospital, and afterward, he made certain to respond thoroughly only to those visitors and staff who had his interest in recovery at heart. The words of others would be countered or deflected so that they could not easily impede his progress.

It is a commonplace that when we search memory for the antecedents of present distress we run across instances of past trauma helplessly and painfully endured. In contrast, when we seek in memory the origins of satisfactory response to trauma, we remember stories told by others that display their unique, actively individual characters responding to difficulty. I am sure I did not read Pearson's story between 1966 and 1988. I did not think of it, of him, or, indeed, of any precedent while I "did it myself" in response to painful trauma. Yet I think Pearson's brick formed part of the path I followed unselfconsciously after the blow to my head.

Pearson's story, and Don Wood's example, stayed in the back of my mind unselfconsciously for more than 20 years before being brought to use spontaneously as a needed learning when the car struck me down. Certain commonalities are evident in their experience and in mine: We all had spontaneous responses to deal with pain and set it aside; an active approach to directing our own treatment; full expressiveness of emotion including sorrow, anger, and humor; a determination to recover quickly and to enjoy life fully; and a watchful eye and clear ear to detect helpful and malign directions from others. All combined to speed healing and to rapidly renew engagement in life.

The Social Nature of the Unconscious Mind

"What a wonderful thing I'm learning. I don't know what I'm saying."
                                        —Student in a hypnotherapy class

In thinking about the "unconscious mind," which is such a central concept in the work of Erickson, Freud, and Jung, I want to present a series of "talking points" that have oriented me in this consideration of my injury and recovery and in a search for its antecedents in my life's experiences.

When I say that Don Wood's and Robert Pearson's stories stayed in my mind "unselfconsciously," I mean that I never forgot or "repressed" them and rarely thought about or consciously referred to them for some 20 years after first hearing them. Unselfconscious knowledge is a great portion of unconscious knowledge. What we call "the wisdom of the body" comprises all the elaborate, organized, unselfconscious neurophysiological processes that sustain life, from respiration and walking to vision and bodily healing. Rossi and Cheek (1988) have made a case for the natural origins of hypnotic therapy in an "ultradian healing response":

> Virtually all the classical phenomena of hypnosis were originally *discovered* as spontaneous manifestations of altered states in everyday life (e.g., daydreaming, sleepwalking, traumatic stress syndrome, etc.). Only after they were so discovered were efforts directed to elicit the phenomena by "suggestion." . . .If we believe that hypnotic phenomena are purely the product of artificial verbal suggestion, then we tend to discount the clinical conception of hypnosis as a *natural psychobiological response to stress and trauma.* (p. 262)

This notion of "unconscious mind" is by turns appealing and frightening. In Freud's view, one might fear the unconscious, which bursts forth in spontaneous neurophysiological events that embarrass (as in parapraxes) or disable (as in the conversion symptoms he treated hypnotically at the beginning of his career). Erickson always assumed that the unconscious mind is a resource into which tangled problems may be dropped and resolved through inner searching of the potentials for action and learned skills held there.

Talking about these unconscious "contents" or "action potentials" is difficult both in the sense that what is unconscious is by definition unsayable, and in the sense that awareness of the unconscious finds no adequate expression in common language. Three attempts have been made to satisfy the demands of the problem of "speaking about the unsayable," or unconscious. One attempt has led to the development of the freakish therapeutic languages, like "object relations," which employ neologisms to speak of unconscious experience. Another attempt involves utilizing natural metaphor and imagery as the appropriate language with which to express the unconscious mind's thought. So: dreams, poetry and gestural language (dance, art) are used to describe and to discuss, or make social, individual unconscious experience. The narrative therapies, such as Epston and White's work (1990), are a modern development of dramatic and metaphorical expression in the use of unconscious social processes to effect change. Again, the paucity of common language terms in English to describe both "internal processes" and social relations of more than two persons makes a metaphorical language such as "storytelling" the language of choice for effective therapies. A third approach, that of Zen Buddhism, substitutes noticing or "pointing" for understanding, and action or gesture for explanation, when expressing "No-mind".

In Jungian approaches, the unconscious mind is conceived of as a repository of the *archetypes of the collective unconscious*: dream images that represent the relations most common to human experience, such as, "mother–son." Interpersonal relations may have expression in this archetypal language: friendship, love, kinship, hypnosis. The single term hides a hyphenated reality: hypnosis = hypnotist–subject, and the noun enfolds a relationship.

Systems of several people, such as groups and families, can best be represented by dreams and family drama or narrative. And social structures, systems of constructed social reality, may also be conceived of as unconscious in this same sense. As Singer (1990) noted: "How strong external social situations are in determining the specific emotion a person feels. It is almost as though the person uses an emotion word to label the evoking situation rather than his specific internal state." (p. 214)

It is as though the specific emotions that came to aid me in constructing a reality of determined effort, expressiveness, and speedy healing after my severe blow to the head and body were the expression of the evoking situation: both the tender concern of the woman who told me, "You're going to be all right," and the pattern laid down by Pearson, Wood, and Erickson in dealing with trauma. My own 20 years' experience in hypnotizing others also helped me to treat myself with the expectation of positive outcome and mobilization of resources that I had encouraged in my patients. In the relationship of a person with his own somatic, emotional, and mental life, stories that lay a pathway to recovery are a great aid. Singer (1990) quotes Silvan Tompkins: "The world we perceive is a dream we learn to have from a script we have not written. It is neither our capricious construction nor a gift we inherit without work." (p. 488)

To summarize: Suppose the interface between neurophysiology and social relations exists within the communication medium we term "hypnosis," as Rossi and Cheek (1988) and many others now suggest. Suppose the concept "unconscious mind" refers to two sets of processes: the unselfconscious organization of human neurophysiology, and the unconscious and unspoken network of social relations. Suppose too that these processes are represented in consciousness by dream images, and emotionally dramatic narratives.

Now suppose further that these unconscious processes are accessed by hypnosis, turmoil, or trauma, and that during a state of dreamy reverie, confusion, or severe shock and surprise, these states accompany the natural formation of representative images and narratives. In hypnotic reverie, confusion, or traumatic surprise, these representations can be expressed in action (as in helpful response to trauma) or selected, combined, and revised (as in the "inner search" of hypnotic therapy). Unselfconscious process appears as a natural, little-known concomitant of ordinary life.

References

Epston, D., & White, M. (1990). *Narrative means to therapeutic ends.* New York: Norton.

Pearson, R. E. (1966). Communication and motivation. *The American Journal of Hypnosis: Clinical, Experimental, Theoretical, 9*(1), 18–25.

Rossi, E. L., & Cheek, D. B. (1988). *Mind-body therapy: Methods of ideodynamic healing in hypnosis.* New York: Norton.

Singer, J. L. (Ed.). (1990). *Repression and dissociation: Implications for personality theory, psychopathology and health.* Chicago: University of Chicago Press.

Managed Care, HMOs, and the Ericksonian Perspective

Michael F. Hoyt, Ph.D.

An Ericksonian perspective, appreciating individuals' capacities and resources within their life-developmental space, will help therapists meet the managed health care challenge of providing satisfying and effective treatments. Commonalities between the essential characteristics of therapy in managed care settings and the defining features of an Ericksonian approach are highlighted, as are several potential difficulties in implementing strategic (and other brief) treatments. It is recommended that therapists working in Health Maintenance Organizations (HMOs) and other managed care arrangements become more familiar with Ericksonian approaches, and that Ericksonian-oriented therapists participate more in professional opportunities within the rapidly expanding managed care field.

I would like to highlight some of the essential parallels between Ericksonian therapy, as I understand it, and the emerging field of managed mental health care. It has been helpful to me to recognize these connections, and it is my hope that as they see essential commonalities, therapists working in health maintenance organizations (HMOs) and other managed care settings will become more familiar with the application of Ericksonian approaches, and that Ericksonian-oriented therapists will participate more in professional opportunities within the managed care movement.

More than 100 million Americans are now covered for mental health services through various forms of managed health care, such as HMOs, preferred providers organizations (PPOs), independent practice associations (IPAs), and employee assistance programs (EAPs) (Austad & Berman, 1991; Austad & Hoyt, 1992; Feldman & Fitzpatrick, 1992; Hoyt, in press;

Address correspondence to Michael F. Hoyt, Ph.D., Department of Psychiatry, Kaiser Permanente Medical Center, 27400 Hersperian Blvd., Hayward, CA 94545.

Hoyt & Austad, 1992). Although "managed care" is a broad, generic term covering great variations in structure and quality, the different forms are all arrangements to regulate the utilization, site, and/or cost of services, the goal being maximal use of limited time and resources. Cutting across various systems and specific therapeutic approaches and extending beyond the single parameter of "brief" or "short-term" are a series of principles that characterize therapy in well-run HMOs and other managed care settings. I will describe them and then trace some connections to the essential characteristics of Ericksonian approaches.

Essential Characteristics of Effective Therapy in Managed Care

1. *Specific problem solving.* The presenting complaint, the reason the patient has now come to therapy, is taken seriously. Effective therapy requires an obtainable goal, and the focus or purpose of treatment may require some negotiation or reframing. The goal is to meet the patient in his or her frame of reference, to use the patient's and therapist's skills to solve the problem that the patient wants solved rather than engaging in a broad, "exploratory" pursuit of putative complexes and "cures."

2. *Rapid response.* Therapy begins immediately, engaging the patient as soon as possible and amplifying useful pretreatment progress (see Hoyt, Rosenbaum & Talmon, 1992).

3. *Clear definition of patient and therapist responsibilities.* The therapist is responsible for appropriately structuring therapeutic contacts, conducting particular interventions, and involving significant other people as needed. The patient is encouraged to participate actively, including carrying out "homework assignments" and implementing behavior changes outside of therapy sessions.

4. *Time is used flexibly and creatively.* The length, frequency, and timing of treatment sessions vary according to patient needs (Hoyt, 1990), with the ideal being the most parsimonious intervention that will be appropriate and likely to have positive effects.

5. *Interdisciplinary cooperation.* Medical and psychological involvement may blend into a more holistic view of the patient. Allied health professionals may participate as indicated, including the use of appropriate psychopharmacology.

6. *Multiple formats and modalities.* Individual, group, and/or family therapy may be used sequentially or concurrently, and participation in various community programs (including 12-step, self-help, and support groups) is vigorously encouraged when appropriate.

7. *Intermittent treatment, or a "family practitioner" model.* The idea of a once-and-for-all "cure" gives way to a more realistic idea that patients can return for "serial" or "distributed" treatment as needed, often focused around developmental issues throughout the life cycle (Budman & Gurman, 1988; Cummings, 1990). The therapist–patient relationship may be long term although frequently abeyant.

8. *Results orientation and accountability.* Is treatment helping? Is it efficacious? (Goodman, Brown, & Deitz, 1992; Kaplan, 1990). Utilization review is undertaken to monitor services and ensure that they are being delivered in the most efficient manner possible to contain costs, and quality assurance procedures are conducted to make sure that the patient is receiving what is needed.

Essential Characteristics of Ericksonian Therapy

What is an "Ericksonian" perspective? What are the defining characteristics that make something "Ericksonian"? A good summary of the major features (or essences) of an Ericksonian approach is provided by Lankton (1990), who identified seven key aspects:

1. *Nonpathology-based model.* Problems are seen as part of, and a result of, attempts at adaptation. Although there can be debate (deShazer, 1990; Fisch, 1990) about whether Erickson construed problems as essentially intrapsychic or in broader systems terms, symptoms are seen as essentially natural (but limiting) responses of unique individuals, "hence, psychotherapy should be formulated to meet the uniqueness of the individual's needs..." (Erickson, in Zeig, 1982, p. vii).

2. *Indirection.* The individual or members of a family are helped to discover talents and resources, options and answers, seemingly without the aid of the therapist.

3. *Utilization.* Whatever the patient brings to the office (understandings, behaviors, motivations) is used as part of the treatment.

4. *Action.* Clients are expected and encouraged to quickly begin to take actions related to the desired goals. This emphasis is a basic ingredient of successful brief therapy regardless of theoretical orientation (Budman, Friedman, and Hoyt, 1992).

5. *Strategy.* Therapists are active in setting or initiating the stages of therapy. The therapist takes responsibility for influencing the patient (Haley, 1973).

6. *Future orientation.* The focus is on action and experience in the present and future rather than the past.

7. *Enchantment.* Treatment engages the mind, appeals to the patient, "captures the ear of the listener" (Gustafson, 1986), and engages "pleasant mental arousal" (Lankton & Lankton, 1986).

Lankton emphasizes that Ericksonian techniques are custom fitted to the needs of the particular case, and notes a number of interventions that are associated with the approach and originated in Erickson's practice: "These include paradoxical assignments, ambiguous function assignments, skill-building assignments, therapeutic metaphors, anecdotes, conscious–unconscious dissociation, hypnotic induction, therapeutic binds, indirect suggestion, and reframing" (1990, p. 366).

All these interventions—hypnosis and strategic assignments and the like—are valuable ways to get people to have experiences that put them in touch with their latent or overlooked abilities, but they are only methods. For Erickson, I think, the basic problem was not pathology or defect but *rigidity*, the idea that people get "stuck" by failing to use a range of skills, competencies, and learnings that they have but are not applying. The basic principle is thus *utilization*, with treatment being personalized to elicit or capitalize on each individual's useful resources. The essential paradigmatic shift is from deficits to strengths, from problems to solutions, from past to future (Fisch, 1990), utilizing whatever the patient brings in the service of healthful change (de Shazer, 1988). The therapy is "constructive" (Hoyt, 1994). As Erickson said: "Patients have problems because their conscious programming has too severely limited their capacities. The solution is to help them break through the limitations of their conscious attitudes to free their unconscious potential for problem solving" (Erickson, Rossi, & Rossi, 1976, p. 18).

The Ericksonian Perspective in the Context of Managed Care

There is already a vast clinical literature, which includes various applications of Ericksonian methods within HMOs (e.g., Budman & Gurman, 1988; Budman, Hoyt, & Friedman, 1992; Chubb, 1983; Friedman & Fanger, 1991; Hoyt, 1990, 1993; Kreilkamp, 1989; Rosenbaum, 1990, 1993; Rosenbaum, Hoyt, & Talmon, 1990; Talmon, 1990). You may already see some of the connections I have in mind—and others that I don't—but let me suggest a few. In the following clinical fragments most of the substance and subtleties of each case—tone, timing, nonverbal communication, and much more—can only be implied. All treatments occurred within the context of a large health maintenance organization, the Kaiser Permanente Medical Center in Hayward, California.

Case One

A man in his eighties was referred by his internist. Various oncology treatments had brought about some unwelcome physical changes and had reduced his vigor. Antidepressant medication had restored some of his energies, but he was demoralized. When my colleague, Norman Weinstein, M.D., and I met with the patient, we learned that he had been the national leader of a large Eastern European church.[1] He had escaped and relocated to the United States just before the crush of Communist rule, and had been a religious prelate in this country as well. He was now semiretired. With recent political developments, he had been invited to return to his native land, where he had not been for many years, for a triumphant reunion at which he would be fêted and asked to deliver an important sermon. He was interested and had his wife's support, but he was so discouraged by his appearance and weakened powers that they were sadly and reluctantly preparing to decline the invitation. Previously a vital and charismatic man, he lamented, "They remember a strong man, but look at me." "Yes, pride is important, especially when you think of how much it would mean to them to see that you have endured and still care for them," we reframed and switched to talking with one another about the beauties of Eastern Europe, the pleasures of speaking one's own language, and the need for spiritual guidance during times of great change. Our patient's ears pricked up. We then asked our patient if he would, at a subsequent appointment, provide us with some relevant Scriptural references to use with demoralized medical patients. Not wanting to appear transparent and not wanting to miss an opportunity for personal growth, we then confessed that our curiosity was more personal—we needed help coming to grips with some adversities in our own lives, including various middle-aged health signals. From his senior perspective, could he offer some guidance? Three more sessions were held, two weeks apart. In each session he read selected Bible passages and discussed them with us in detail. Treatment was effective: we felt encouraged, and the patient made his journey back home. At a follow-up visit upon his return he reported that the trip had been very satisfying, successful, and at times quite arduous. His eyes twinkled. He acknowledged our "good care," as he graciously called it, and appropriately added, "Thank God I went!"

---

[1]As my colleague Robert Rosenbaum, Ph.D. (1992, personal communication), has noted, having others available for consultation and co-therapy can be an advantage of working in an HMO, although arrangements have to be made; otherwise there is seldom enough time for extended discussion or treatment planning.

Case Two

A couple came in with their 19-year-old son, a college student who lived at home with them. As they had been for some time, they were all arguing about curfews, discipline, "respecting the rules of the house," and the like. When asked if I had any children, I gestured to a photograph on the desk of my son, "who's still little and dependent, since he's only five," and went on to talk about a bird's nest we had seen and how smart Mother Nature was the way she designed things, like how it worked that a little bird would stay in its nest but when it got big enough to make things crowded in the nest it was big enough to fly on its own and so its readiness to go was built in and signaled by its size and neither the grown-up birds nor the grown-up bird needed to be told or could help it, since it was natural, etc., etc. I prattled on for a bit, sort of like an ornithological Lt. Colombo, and finally stopped myself. I shifted around in my chair, seemingly pulling myself together and returning to the topic at hand. "It's nice to see such a loving, close family. So, who's going to finally give in?" I asked, and pursued a line of questioning that only escalated the fight and demonstrated the intractability of the conflict. A follow-up phone call six weeks later revealed that a week after the session, everyone had agreed that it would be best if the son lived elsewhere. Everyone was happy. We'll never know, but the bird's nest metaphor with its various embedded suggestions seemed to prefigure and guide their conflict resolution in a developmentally appropriate direction. The "empty nest syndrome" was better than the "overcrowded nest syndrome."

Case Three

A woman sought therapy to overcome her great anxiety when driving across bridges, a problem that can be of considerable inconvenience for someone living in the San Francisco Bay area. The conventional cognitive-behavioral relaxation-and-gradual-exposure treatment was potentiated by a number of Ericksonian-type interventions (see Feldman, 1988). Her attention was refocused first through "splitting the symptom" by dividing a bridge into boringly small segments, and later by having her mentally "compress" a bridge trip into "mere seconds" while greatly expanding the attention given to the pleasures beyond the bridges (such as visiting grandchildren and shopping). "Pseudo-orientation in time" (Erickson, 1954) was used, having the patient repeatedly visualize and describe aloud various bridges as they would appear from the far side in the near future when she was at ease. Because she wanted the best treatment, we were able to persuade her that more data would be necessary about her reactions at different times and locations, and so she needed to begin driving—sometimes quite anxiously—across several bridges at varying times of day and night. This experiment—which was designed to put the cure before the treatment—promoted her desensitizing exposure and convinced her that she could drive with reasonable comfort so long as she could avoid the "ordeal" (Haley, 1984) of rush-hour traffic.

Case Four

Requests for psychological consultation from a medical-surgical ward sometimes come when the patient–caregiver cooperation that good healthcare requires is disrupted (Hoyt, Opsvig, & Weinstein, 1981). Such was the situation involving a hospitalized medical patient whose many anxious demands for attention had finally overtaxed her nurses' sympathies. They were certainly not neglecting her, but after making many visits to her room without seeing any medical urgency, they were busy attending to other patients, a situation that resulted in the patient feeling abandoned and increasingly anxious. She was almost constantly activating her call light, and the situation was escalating. The level of mutual irritation was temporarily so high that simple reassurance to the patient and a direct request to the nurses for extraordinary goodwill and increased attention were not likely to succeed. The patient was offered a small dose of tranquilizing medication, which she accepted, and an order was written for the nurses to check the patient's vital signs every 15 minutes. Prescribing "kind hand-holding" was not likely to succeed, but this indirection resulted in the patient's being repeatedly and gently attended to, including physical contact as her heart sounds, blood pressure, and pulse were taken. This attention, combined with the medication, soothed the patient (Auer, 1988; Goldsmith, 1988). After two hours peace and cooperation were restored, and the special nursing orders were discontinued. The remainder of the patient's hospital stay presented no special problems.

Case Five

A woman arrived in our emergency room in a somewhat hysterical state, transported by an ambulance from a nearby medical clinic, where her family had taken her. When I arrived at the ER, the physician on duty warned me that "It's going to be a long night." Meaning well, he was eager to administer diazepam (Valium) but had held off pending psychiatric consultation. A paramedic was with the patient in an examination room attempting to talk with her. I glanced in and saw that although not as upset as she apparently had been when she first arrived, she was still quite overwrought. The paramedic continued trying to calm her while I sought the husband in the waiting room.

He seemed to be a reasonable and sympathetic fellow and related a recent complicated family history of escalating conflict. A sister-in-law had demanded a large personal loan from the patient—which she had refused as both unreasonable and financially impossible—and the sister-in-law had, since that time, been making various accusations and vindictively attempting to turn family members against the patient. Described by her husband as "very sensitive" and "close to her family," the patient had found this very distressing. A few hours before arriving in our ER, she had received from her antagonist a threatening letter with an announcement of plans for a lawsuit. At this news, she "snapped." She had been crying uncontrollably, shaking, and unable to walk when her family took her to the medical clinic near their home.

The husband indicated that the patient's father, father-in-law, and mother-in-law were all concerned and present at the ER. "Will seeing you calm her or just get her more upset?" I asked. He assured me that he could talk with her if given a chance without family interference. I got the paramedic out of the room, thanked him, and brought in the husband. The wife started to get more upset, but I raised my hand and quickly said, "Stop! I have an important question." She hesitated, and I asked quickly, "Is this your husband? He says he's been married to you for 15 years. Is that true?" She nodded, and I continued: "Do you love him? Does he love you? Will you let him talk with you in a way to help you?" Her emotional "roll" was disrupted. The "yeses" tumbled out. I then further distracted the patient from her distress with some banter about the plumbing in the ER (the husband was a plumber by trade), got them both laughing, and then asked her, "Is he a good guy?" When she answered positively, I quickly said to the husband, "Good. I knew you were the right man for the case. I'll leave you two alone," and departed, pulling the curtain.

A few minutes later when I checked she was somewhat less distressed, and they were having a heart-to-heart talk. I chatted up the ER doctor to buy some time. In another 15 minutes the husband emerged and asked if the father and in-laws could see her. He and I got them. I let the husband do most of the talking. When they asked, "Doctor, is she all right?" I said, "She's OK but is very upset because she thinks you're mad at her and hate her." They protested and strongly indicated their love and concern. The husband encouraged them to express these feelings to her. As we walked into the patient's room I announced, "There are some people here who love you and want to talk with you. It's nice to see such a good family," and I left. In about 15 minutes I looked in. Something had happened. Tears and hugs were in evidence all around the room. "I knew this wasn't a case for a doctor," I remarked. "It's a case for the love of a family." They appreciated the recognition. One half hour later the patient and her family, happily reunited, left the ER. On the way out the husband shook my hand. "You did a great job," I said, and thanked him. As in Erickson's famous story of returning the stray horse by simply keeping things on track (Gordon, 1978), the key was remembering to use the available family resources and to stay out of nature's way.

Resolving the so-called presenting complaint, directing treatment so that the patient rapidly becomes engaged in therapeutic activities, using patients' capacities, meeting flexibly within an intermittent treatment model, and paying keen attention to what works and to getting the job done are features of both Ericksonian and managed care work. As Kristina Erickson (1988) has written, careful attention must be paid to the three principles of proper evaluation and creative planning, cultivating and assuring patient commitment, and emphasizing patient strengths and tailoring treatment to the individual.

Barriers to Brief Therapy

There are various general problems or difficulties in doing brief therapy, including the need to overcome or suspend the self-fulfilling long-term treatment assumptions of much traditional psychotherapy training, the demands for greater therapist alertness and focused activity, potential financial and emotional disincentives, and termination problems that stem from frequent attachment and letting go (Hoyt, 1985, 1990, 1991, in press).

Doing so-called Ericksonian strategic or naturalistic therapy has some added potential disadvantages that Johnson (1988, pp. 411–412) has noted: (a) unnatural, sometimes nonintuitive behavior is required from the therapist; (b) for most of us, strategic-type therapy often requires consultative help—Kristina Erickson's comments (1988, p. 383) about seeing her father spend hours preparing a particular intervention are instructive; (c) there is still relatively little professional support for strategic interventions, which may be seen by the uninitiated as "strange" or "unconventional" and disruptive (exactly!);[2] (d) your patients will give you less credit, which tends to happen when you do minimalist interventions that empower patients rather than promoting their dependency and your authority (see Talmon, Hoyt, & Rosenbaum, 1990); and (e) if you do this kind of work long enough, you begin to have some successes with patients with whom other therapists did not succeed, the result being that you get referred more and more "hard" cases while others get or keep the relatively "easy" ones. As the

---

[2]Along related lines, see Sluzki's discussion (1992) of the profound institutional impact that can result when there is a shift to a more collaborative and egalitarian solution-oriented patient–provider relationship.

managed care field evolves, however, I expect that effective therapists will be rewarded with more referrals of all types, and the utilization review process will be reduced so that clinicians known for their competencies will be able to proceed without undue interference. Standards of care and accountability are important, lest ineffective or even destructive practices be tolerated in the name of "trusting the unconscious" (Hoyt, 1989). Still, recently re-reading O'Hanlon and Hexum's wonderful compendium, *An Uncommon Casebook: The Complete Clinical Works of Milton H. Erickson, M.D.* (1990), I chuckled at the thought of Dr. Erickson's having to provide DSM-III-R diagnoses and explain his treatment plans to justify "preauthorization of services"!

Bridges to the Future

Psychological practice in the 1990s is, and will continue to be, increasingly influenced by financial forces (Cummings, 1986; Zimet, 1989). Consistent with the principles of therapy in managed care settings and especially compatible with the HMO ideal of *health* maintenance are parsimonious treatments that strategically amplify and utilize clients' healthful resources and responses. Assisting clients to achieve their self-defined goals through the facilitation of present- and future-oriented actions and experience increases the cooperative nature of treatment and, hence, the likelihood of therapeutic efficiency (K. Erickson, 1988; Lankton, 1990; Zeig, 1990). The characteristics and goals of HMO practice and Ericksonian therapy are highly congruent, including the orientation toward problem solving, the involvement of patients in their own care, the emphasis on a life-cycle or developmental model, and the use of interdisciplinary cooperation and treatment planning. HMOs and related managed care settings should provide fertile ground for the application of the Ericksonian perspective.

References

Auer, J. (1988). Ericksonian hypnosis and psychotherapy in clinical settings. In S. R. Lankton & J. K. Zeig (Eds.). *Ericksonian monographs, No. 4: Research, comparisons, and medical applications of Ericksonian techniques.* New York: Brunner/Mazel.

Austad, C. S., & Berman, W. H. (Eds.). (1991). *Psychotherapy in managed health care: The optimal use of time and resources.* Washington, DC: American Psychological Association.

Austad, C. S., & Hoyt, M. F. (1992). The managed care movement and the future of psychotherapy. *Psychotherapy, 29,* 109–118.

Budman, S. H., Friedman, S., & Hoyt, M. F. (1992). Last words on first sessions. In S. H. Budman, M. F. Hoyt, & S. Friedman (Eds.), *The first session in brief therapy* (pp. 345–358). New York: Guilford.

Budman, S. H., & Gurman, A. S. (1988). *Theory and practice of brief therapy.* New York: Guilford.
Budman, S. H., Hoyt, M. F., & Friedman, S. (Eds.). (1992). *The first session in brief therapy.* New York: Guilford.
Chubb, H. (1983). Interactional brief therapy: Child problems in an HMO clinic. *Journal of Strategic and Systemic Therapy, 2,* 70–76.
Cummings, N. A. (1986). The dismantling of our health care system: Strategies for the survival of psychological practice. *American Psychologist, 41,* 426–431.
Cummings, N. A. (1990). Brief intermittent psychotherapy throughout the life cycle. In J. K. Zeig & S. G. Gilligan (Eds.), *Brief therapy: Myths, methods and metaphors* (pp. 169–184). New York: Brunner/Mazel.
de Shazer, S. (1988). *Clues: Investigating solutions in brief therapy.* New York: Norton.
de Shazer, S. (1990). Erickson's systemic perspective. In S. R. Lankton (Ed.), *Ericksonian monographs, No. 7: The broader implications of Ericksonian therapy* (pp. 6–8). New York: Brunner/Mazel.
Erickson, K. K. (1988). One method for designing short-term intervention-oriented Ericksonian therapy. In J. K. Zeig & S. R. Lankton (Eds.), *Developing Ericksonian therapy* (pp. 379–396). New York: Brunner/Mazel.
Erickson, M. (1954). Pseudo-orientation in time as a hypnotherapeutic procedure. *Journal of Clinical and Experimental Hypnosis, 2,* 261–283.
Erickson, M. H., Rossi, E., & Rossi, S. (1976). *Hypnotic realities.* New York: Irvington.
Feldman, J. B. (1988). The utilization of cognition in psychotherapy: A comparison of Ericksonian and cognitive therapies. In S. R. Lankton & J. K. Zeig (Eds.), *Ericksonian monographs, No. 4* (pp. 57–73). New York: Brunner/Mazel.
Feldman, J. L., & Fitzpatrick, R. J. (Eds.). (1992). *Managed mental health care: Administrative and clinical issues.* Washington, DC: American Psychiatric Press.
Fisch, R. (1990). The broader implications of Milton H. Erickson's work. In S. R. Lankton (Ed.), *Ericksonian monographs, No. 7* (pp. 1–5). New York: Brunner/Mazel.
Friedman, S., & Fanger M. T. (1991). *Expanding therapeutic possibilities: Getting results in brief psychotherapy.* New York: Lexington Books/Macmillan.
Goldsmith, S. (1988). The application of Ericksonian principles to the use of medication. In S. R. Lankton & J. K. Zeig (Eds.), *Ericksonian monographs, No. 4* (pp. 91–99). New York: Brunner/Mazel.
Goodman, M., Brown, J., & Deitz, P. (1992). *Managing managed care: A mental health practitioner's survival guide.* Washington, DC: American Psychiatric Press.
Gordon, D. (1978). *Therapeutic metaphors.* Cupertino, CA: Meta Publications.
Gustafson, J. P. (1986). *The complex secret of brief psychotherapy.* New York: Norton.
Haley, J. (1973). *Uncommon therapy: The psychiatric techniques of Milton H. Erickson, M.D.* New York: Norton.
Haley, J. (1984). *Ordeal therapy.* New York: Norton.
Hoyt, M. F. (1985). Therapist resistance to short-term dynamic psychotherapy. *Journal of the American Academy of Psychoanalysis, 13,* 93–112.
Hoyt, M. F. (1989). Letter to the editor. *The Milton H. Erickson Foundation newsletter, 9* (1), 5.
Hoyt, M. F. (1990). On time in brief therapy. In R. A. Wells & V. J. Giannetti (Eds.), *Handbook of the brief psychotherapies* (pp. 115–143). New York: Plenum.
Hoyt, M. F. (1991). Teaching and learning short-term psychotherapy in an HMO. In C. S. Austad & W. H. Berman (Eds.), *Psychotherapy in managed health care* (pp. 98–107). Washington, DC: American Psychological Association.

Hoyt, M. F. (1993). Two cases of brief therapy in an HMO. In R. A. Wells & V. J. Giannetti (Eds.), *Casebook of the brief psychotherapies* (pp. 235–248). New York: Plenum.

Hoyt, M. F. (Ed.). (1994). *Constructive therapies.* New York: Guilford.

Hoyt, M. F. (in press). *Brief therapy and managed care: Selected papers.* San Francisco: Jossey-Bass.

Hoyt, M. F., & Austad, C. S. (1992). Psychotherapy in a staff-model health maintenance organization: Providing and assuring quality care in the future. *Psychotherapy, 29,* 119–129.

Hoyt, M. F., Opsvig, P., & Weinstein, N. W. (1981). Conjoint patient–staff interview in hospital case management. *International Journal of Psychiatry in Medicine, 11,* 83–87.

Hoyt, M. F., Rosenbaum, R., & Talmon, M. (1992). Planned single-session psychotherapy. In S. H. Budman, M. F. Hoyt, & S. Friedman (Eds.), *The first session in brief therapy* (pp. 59–86). New York: Guilford.

Johnson, L. D. (1988). Naturalistic techniques with the "difficult" patient. In J. K. Zeig & S. R. Lankton (Eds.), *Developing Ericksonian therapy* (pp. 397–413). New York: Brunner/Mazel.

Kaplan, J. G. (1989). Efficacy: The real bottom line in health care. *HMO Practice, 3,* 108–110.

Kreilkamp, T. (1989). *Time-limited intermittent therapy with children and families.* New York: Brunner/Mazel.

Lankton, C. R., & Lankton, S. R. (1986). *Tales of enchantment: Goal-oriented metaphors for adults and children in therapy.* New York: Brunner/Mazel.

Lankton, S. R. (1990). Ericksonian strategic therapy. In J. K. Zeig & W. M. Munion (Eds.), *What is psychotherapy? Contemporary perspectives* (pp. 363–371). San Francisco: Jossey-Bass.

O'Hanlon, W. H., & Hexum, A. L. (1990). *An uncommon casebook: The complete clinical work of Milton H. Erickson, M.D.* New York: Norton.

Rosenbaum, R. (1990). Strategic psychotherapy. In R. A. Wells & V. J. Giannetti (Eds.), *Handbook of the brief psychotherapies* (pp. 351–403). New York: Plenum.

Rosenbaum, R. (1993). Heavy ideals: Strategic single-session hypnotherapy. In R. A. Wells & V. J. Giannetti (Eds.), *Casebook of the brief psychotherapies* (pp. 109–128). New York: Plenum.

Rosenbaum, R., Hoyt, M. F., & Talmon, M. (1990). The challenge of single-session therapies: Creating pivotal moments. In R. A. Wells & V. J. Giannetti (Eds.), *Handbook of the brief psychotherapies* (pp. 165–189). New York: Plenum.

Sluzki, C. E. (1992). Foreword. In B. Furman & T. Ahola, *Solution talk: Hosting therapeutic conversations.* New York: Norton.

Talmon, M. (1990). *Single-session therapy: Maximizing the effect of the first (and often only) therapeutic encounter.* San Francisco: Jossey-Bass.

Talmon, M., Hoyt, M. F., & Rosenbaum, R. (1990). Effective single-session therapy: Step-by-step guidelines. In M. Talmon, *Single-session therapy* (pp. 34–56). San Francisco: Jossey-Bass.

Zeig, J. K. (Ed.). (1982). *Ericksonian approaches to hypnosis and psychotherapy.* New York: Brunner/Mazel.

Zeig, J. K. (1990). Ericksonian psychotherapy. In J. K. Zeig & W. M. Munion (Eds.), *What is psychotherapy? Contemporary perspectives* (pp. 371–377). San Francisco: Jossey-Bass.

Zimet, C. N. (1989). The mental health revolution: Will psychology survive? *American Psychologist, 44,* 703–708.

Ericksonian Approaches to Curiosity in the Treatment of Incest and Sexual Abuse Survivors

Paula J. Haymond, Ed.D.

Although much has been written about the variety of applications of Milton Erickson's treatment techniques and style, one of the most seminal aspects of his work is his curiosity about his own life and the lives of his patients. Erickson's demonstration of curiosity has been viewed as a given in the literature but has not received attention as a topic in itself. Curiosity is of compelling importance as an agent of change in Ericksonian therapy. The expression of such curiosity and the engenderment of curiosity in a patient immediately allow the patient and the therapist to join in common cause, to engage together in creative problem solving. Specifically, in the treatment of incest and sexual abuse survivors, such curiosity allows a patient to be interested in the environment rather than afraid of it, to be able to experience pleasure in current life more strongly than the pain of memories, and to be able to lay the foundation for future learnings rather than hiding from life's diversity in rigidly defined repetitions. This paper explains the purpose served by curiosity in therapy and provides two treatment vignettes by way of illustration.

Books, articles, and journals dedicated to the treatment of incest and sexual abuse have inundated public awareness during the last ten years. The telling of survivors' stories in all forms of media has forced us to recognize that incest is more widespread than we wished to believe and crosses social, economic, and racial boundaries. Only a few such cases are reported in Milton Erickson's writings, and in these cases incest and sexual abuse were rarely, if ever, the presenting problem. Erickson did, however, frequently deal with sexual dysfunction and the directing of individuals toward normal sexual development through creative learning approaches.

Address correspondence to Paula J. Haymond, Ed.D., 812 Hawthorne, Houston, TX 77006.

Erickson extended himself to tailor therapy to the individual's needs. He went out to dinner with patients, had patients in his home to meet other people of interest, and instructed patients in how to go about improving the quality of their lives. Curiosity, as a primary motivator in helping a patient learn new behavior, is at the heart of Erickson's teachings. However, a survey of the literature reveals no direct discussion of this key principle. Using the patient's natural curiosity to bring about learning of new ways of healthy functioning in the midst of dealing with incest and sexual abuse issues is the topic of this paper. This use of curiosity as a creative learning tool proves to be a natural utilization of Erickson's approaches to treatment.

Sexual Abuse

Russell (1986), in her work *The Secret Trauma: Incest in Lives of Girls and Women,* reported the results of her extensive survey of 930 women. Incestuous abuse as defined in Russell's survey was divided into four levels, including:

[1] any kind of exploitive sexual contact or attempted contact that occurred between relatives, no matter how distant the relationship, before the victim turned 18 years of age; [2] unwanted sexual experiences with persons unrelated by blood or marriage, ranging from attempted petting (touching of breasts or genitals or attempts at such touching) to rape, before the victim turned 14 years, and completed or attempted forcible rape experiences from the ages of 14 to 17 years (inclusive); [3] less severe experiences of extrafamilial child sexual abuse...for example unwanted kisses, hugs and other nongenital touching; [4] experiences with exhibitionists as well as other unwanted noncontact sexual experiences. (Russell, 1986, pp. 59–62)

Under this broader definition, "54% (N=504) reported at least one experience of incestuous and/or extrafamilial sexual abuse before they reached 18 years of age, and 48% (N=450) reported at least one such experience before they reached 14 years of age." Narrower definitions of sexual abuse yielded "38% (N=357) of the women being incested and/or extrafamilialy sexually abused before the age of 18 and 28% (N=258) before the age of 14" (Russell, 1986, p. 60).

Projecting these figures onto the population at large suggests that incest and extrafamilial sexual abuse represent a major source of trauma for women. Sexual abuse has been reported in approximately two to nine percent of males. These figures are believed to be a gross underestimation of sexual abuse among young males (Courtois, 1988, p. 16). Although men also have been victims and survivors of incest and sexual abuse, the focus of this paper will remain on women.

Van der Kolk (1987) suggests in his work *Psychological Trauma* that diagnosing post traumatic stress disorder among incest survivors is often complicated by an overlay of other symptoms. "The underlying problem often is obscured by chronic depression, self-destructive behavior, and drug and alcohol abuse" (p. 17). Others have tried to enumerate symptoms of incest and sexual abuse, and these lists grow longer and at times more contradictory with each attempt. Common features do seem to emerge among incest survivors that perhaps are unique to this group of trauma patients. Chronic depression with recurring thoughts of suicide, or suicidal behavior, emerges frequently. Dissociation, which plays a major role in the emotional/psychological coping of the patient, appears to form an alliance with underlying suicidal impulses at times leading to a general lack of awareness of safety issues. Many of these women seem to lack a basic awareness of "how to survive," sometimes to the extent of failing to maintain focus on day-to-day living skills.

Ericksonian Perspectives

Ericksonian therapy provides a variety of perspectives from which to view the many ways in which an individual might be guided toward healthier, more pleasurable living. Adopting this creative learning approach helps patients break free of their learned limitations and discover their underlying potential. The therapist's willingness to join in the patient's reality is essential as an avenue for building sufficient trust within the relationship to allow the patient to risk changing. One way Erickson repeatedly demonstrated this process of joining was to become immersed in the language of his patients. He then utilized this joining to set the stage for a sudden and unexpected breaking out of the patient's language set, thereby opening a new pathway for learning.

For the incest survivor, the acceptance and validation of her experiences and memories can provide the first step of moving the therapist into the patient's reality. Yet it is the therapist's responsibility to be aware of what developmental experiences have been missed, twisted, or overutilized and, therefore, are in need of normalization. Often such maladaptive developmental experiences are motivated by the survivor's past and continuing fears and terrors. Erickson's learning approaches foster curiosity rather than fear of the environment, moving the individual toward a greater capacity to feel and experience the pleasure of being alive, while establishing the foundation for future learnings. The therapeutic use of curiosity also allows for the clarification of the patient's mislearnings about life through participation in a nonthreatening relationship, which is accompanied by experiences aimed at remediating inaccurate self-perceptions, interpersonal misunderstandings, and developmental misinformation.

Ericksonian hypnosis can be utilized in the treatment of sexual dysfunction. The hypnotic process can provide a framework for building a sense of internal and external safety, it can reframe events by drawing on a broader range of experiences within the individual's behavioral and mnemonic repertoire, and it can aid in the working through of unconscious material in a less traumatic way. Yet, formal trance work with some survivors may prove to be too destabilizing. Erickson, in *Life Reframing in Hypnosis* (1985), states:

> Another general matter I want to impress upon you concerns awareness. Is it really necessary for your patient to know that he is hypnotized? Does it serve any good purpose for either you or your patient to know that you put him in a trance? What does the patient really need? He primarily needs the responsiveness and receptiveness of the hypnotic state. . . .too often. . .the effort is made to get the patient to recognize too much about the trance state. Too much effort is made to direct his critical faculties toward ascertaining the degree of hypnosis rather than directing his interest to the accomplishment of the purposes of the hypnosis. (pp. 147–148)

One way to understand Erickson's statement is to note the important contributions he made with the demonstration and refinement of the naturalistic trance. Utilization of naturalistic trance states with incest survivors is likely to prove more productive than formal trance induction, especially with those individuals whose ability to maintain contact with the present is tenuous. People who have poor ego boundaries or decompensate in response to their own internal promptings are often poor candidates for formal hypnosis, in which dissociation is frequently reinforced. With a naturalistic approach, distraction, fixation, and generalization can be accomplished by one or two sentences embedded within the ongoing session. The individual's response to suggestions can be quickly monitored, and nonproductive reactions immediately addressed. The creativity occurs as the individual breaks from past patterns of responding and becomes aware that there are ways of responding that before now have not been experienced.

Once the individual develops an awareness of the broad array of possible responses to life experiences, the exploration of those possibilities becomes the focus of learning. Curiosity plays a primary role in moving the individual toward more creative problem solving. It is evidenced in spontaneous surprise experiences in which affect and intellect are wholly integrated. Puzzlement or confusion is suddenly replaced by a surprising understanding accompanied by a sense of pleasure, satisfaction and perhaps even humor. This actually leads beyond the development of insight or introspection because it catalyzes an increased desire for more surprises, healthy pleasures, and, thus, more learnings. Insight represents the pulling forward of past experiences into an understanding of how the past affects the present. Curiosity fosters the pull of the individual toward a future containing the wonder, pleasure, and amusement that accompany the uncovering of even more pleasant surprises.

Adopting an attitude of curiosity toward an experience reframes that experience automatically. It removes preconceived ideas about the experience so that other outcomes may arise. Erickson demonstrated the use of curiosity when he invited the patient to look at the numerous variations seen in nature. In one case he prescribed asking a patient to spend an hour watching the grass grow and then to report what he learned from the experience (Rosen, 1982, p. 186). His instructions to the patient are filled with his own curiosity and the clear expectation that this assignment would be surprisingly meaningful to the patient.

The balance required in learning about surprises and uncovering the secrets of life facilitates creative moments in which positive growth can occur. Erickson postulates that "every time you surprise a small child you widen his range of responses" (Erickson & Rossi, 1979, pp. 376–377). For the incest survivor, the whole realm of surprises and secrets has been spoiled. Erickson further states, "When you keep a secret, you widen your understanding of how things work" (Erickson & Rossi, 1979, pp. 376–377). Surprise, for the incest survivor, has become an element of how one might unexpectedly be abused. For the incest survivor, secrets have become wrapped in the shame of abuse, severely restricting how she perceives experiences and relates to her environment. She fails to learn about the healthy excitement of holding on to a positive secret until disclosure is appropriate. She has not learned that sometimes disclosing the secret can be even more exhilarating than the actual contents of the secret itself. Everyone has seen how very difficult it is for a small child to keep the secret of a gift bought for a loved one. The difficulty is containing the child's excitement. The glee a child experiences over the opening of the present encompasses that healthy experience of having learned how to keep a secret.

Erickson notes that "one must widen a whole lot of receptors to uncover a secret" (Erickson & Rossi, 1979, pp. 376–377). For the incest survivor, uncovering secrets often becomes a frightening and painful task. It is typically focused on recovering memories and experiences of abuse; as a result, the present pain and discomfort are fitted into a past framework of more pain and discomfort. Learning becomes a retrospective study of the abuses she has experienced. Learning about life becomes centered around the unconscious or conscious understandings of her abuse, shame, and fear. The ability to experience curiosity as a motivating force for creative and pleasurable learning is at best limited and at worst lost altogether.

Erickson also states, "Every time you try to keep a secret, you have to find ways of hiding it. That's an important learning process too. Just keeping a secret makes you learn to erect guards, defenses. It broadens all of your understanding to keep a secret" (Erickson & Rossi, 1979, pp. 376–377). In the course of normal development, learning to keep secrets entails appropriate learnings about interpersonal boundaries: you might tell one person one thing about yourself, while withholding that information from another person. It teaches the right time to disclose the content of a secret; then the understanding that the environment may or may not be supportive of such disclosure; and finally the process of deciding how to reveal the secret. An incest survivor generally demonstrates poor understanding of interpersonal boundaries, impulse control, and timing. Her coping mechanisms are primarily focused on past patterns of learned limitations. The experience of surprise becomes rigidly and narrowly defined as destructive. Learning about herself, relationships, and her environment is restricted to these areas where venturing beyond these limitations poses the least threat emotionally, psychologically, and physically. The realm of possible interactions is now circumscribed by her learned and subsequently self-imposed limitations. Her ability to keep secrets becomes restricted to the keeping of horrifying secrets about her abuse. Sometimes the secrets are even kept from herself. The repression of memories drains off psychological energy and limits access to her unconscious resources, thus reducing her ability to meet the demands for adequate functioning in the present.

Sparking the curiosity of an incest survivor can often initiate broad changes. Therapeutic interventions designed to instill a sense of wonderment within the patient can open the door for enduring and dramatic lifestyle changes. If the patient's sense of curiosity is facilitated and enhanced, her limited responses are replaced with readiness and expectancy for more positive life experiences. Therapists must adopt within themselves a congruent state of pleased and interested expectancy as patients move toward deeper levels of curiosity. The more curious the therapist is about life and its mysteries, the easier it is to convey to the patient this attitude about learning of excited and pleased expectancy of pleasure. The concept of life itself is thereby reframed from being a rigid, painful and predictable pattern into being a series of fluid and surprising learnings. The therapist fosters curiosity untainted by preconceived notions of outcomes, which focuses on the infinite variety of possible outcomes that can be derived from unrestricted positive learning experiences.

In the following case studies, inviting the patient to become curious about all aspects of her life becomes the central theme of treatment. Such an approach helps the incest survivor to rediscover her innate ability to reframe past experiences, move more successfully into the present, and define a future orientation to continue her personal, social, and sexual growth.

Case One

Eve is a 30-year-old widow who sought treatment after terminating with her previous therapist, who had facilitated the recollection of incest and sexual abuse memories. This therapist had referred her. Eve admitted to suicidal ideation and preoccupation but denied intent. She described herself as "addicted to suicidal thinking," and she was unable to resolve even day-to-day issues without reverting to these thoughts. She denied having made any suicide attempts but had episodically hoarded a variety of pills and at one point had purchased a gun. In the intervening years before this initial interview, she had safely disposed of both. However, she frequently thought of purchasing a gun again. Despite graduate training in counseling, numerous years of continuous treatment with psychiatrists, and multiple hospitalizations, Eve remained marginally adjusted. She reported being extremely distressed by her incest memories. Eve initially appeared highly motivated toward therapy, not in the direction of working through these experiences but, rather, toward uncovering more memories, which continued to feed suicidal thinking, poor self-esteem, and repeated episodes of rage and depression. Her expression of curiosity had become self-victimizing.

The initial treatment sessions we will address here focused on establishing her basic safety needs. She exercised at night in unlit areas of an urban center. This exercising consisted of running beyond her physical limits, resulting in frequent physical injuries. Injuries did not stop her from exercising; on the contrary, they tended to ignite further exercising to demonstrate that she could endure pain. Patient–therapist contracts were agreed upon to address the issues of compulsive overexercise, sleeplessness, and improper nutrition. Specifically, she agreed to limit exercise to one-mile daylight walks. A bedtime hour was set, and regular meals were mutually agreed upon. The last two points never had been a part of her self-care, and needed to become well integrated into her newly evolving lifestyle.

As Eve accepted these contractual changes into her daily life, she gradually became interested in broadening her horizons: exercising in new locations, trying new items and locations for meals, and experimenting with bedtime rituals. Her meals were eventually adjusted to accommodate morning and afternoon social contacts. Her sleeping was facilitated through experimentation with finding different ways to make herself comfortable. Focus was taken off suicidal thinking and turned toward building basic living skills.

Throughout the course of the therapeutic relationship, fears of abandonment and rejection required continued attention. To facilitate trust in the relationship, to improve object constancy, and to focus her awareness on something outside her emotional pain, a transitional object was lent to her. Eve was both pleased and surprised when a stuffed dragon was given to her to care for between sessions. Eve's questions regarding the meaning or purpose of the dragon were met with pleased expectancy but no explanation. Eve pondered the rationale for the action, and the responsibilities involved. Eve's ambivalence toward the dragon was stated in terms of its interfering with her suicidal thinking and planning. Over the course of treatment, the pleasure she took in developing the skills and confidence in caring for the toy became more apparent. This tactic was especially useful over long weekends, when she had difficulty maintaining object constancy. She was encouraged to take the stuffed animal with her everywhere. She could do this by concealing the toy in a bag or by leaving it in her car. In those situations where she felt comfortable, she could even carry the toy openly. These activities later helped her to become more flexible in her willingness to carry out tasks that were more abstract.

Over the course of several months, she divulged that she often had wanted to have a dog, but felt too inadequate to care for it properly. She also felt that it would interfere with her ability to carry out any suicidal thinking by requiring her to think of how she would take care of the dog. Her childhood memories of dogs were among the few positive experiences she could recall. Utilizing Erickson's approach of moving the individual toward healthier, productive pleasures, it was suggested seven months into treatment that she could probably have a dog, but that she wasn't quite ready. The time wasn't exactly right, but perhaps in the spring it would be just the right time. This future-oriented suggestion projected an image and an expectation of a future in which she would know she had the ability to care for a dog. Erickson used this approach in dealing with growing-up issues such as being old enough to eat spinach, and wondering how many stitches his youngest son would get to have and would it be more than his siblings had gotten when they had been injured.

Work continued to focus on taking care of basic needs. She lost her first job and got another one during this time, curtailed all contact with her abusive family, and moved into an apartment where keeping a dog would be allowed. She became increasingly curious about the possibilities of owning a dog and imagined having fun and pleasure with about a half dozen different breeds of dogs. The anticipation and building expectancy of the future pleasure of owning a dog became a powerful competitor to her ritualized suicidal thinking. During this time, treatment focused on passive-aggressive behaviors and her continued difficulties with authority figures, including, but not limited to, her therapist. In the spring she was encouraged to begin the process of looking for a dog. Contracts were constructed around Eve's researching and learning about different breeds of dogs, visiting local kennels, conferring with local dog trainers, and attending a dog show to see, touch, and experience all sorts of dogs. She became more excited about the prospect of ownership as the weeks passed. At one point she could no longer contain her impulsivity and adopted a four-year-old Doberman pinscher. Unfortunately, the dog turned out to have very little bite inhibition and became extremely intimidating and territorial in her home. After a week of trying to convinced herself this dog was pleasing to own, she relented and returned the dog to the breeder. In the therapy session, this experience was reframed in terms of learning about timing and impulse control. It also allowed her the opportunity to explore different breeds of dogs which by nature were more friendly, loving, and outgoing. In late spring she adopted a three-year-old black Labrador retriever who was affectionate and lovable.

Shortly afterward, she lost her second job. Her depression and suicidal thinking resurfaced but the quality was quite different. Suicide planning now had to include the care of her dog. During this period of unemployment, treatment focused on the relationship she was building with her dog. Sessions were spent encouraging her to make small, safe ventures into the world of dog ownership. She received reinforcement in the form of pleased expectancy, and supportive interpretations, and was subtly guided in her curiosity toward watching how the dog behaved in new versus familiar situations, how he communicated with her, and how she responded to his needs. Because this relationship provided the majority of pleasure in her life, she was instructed to carry out more daily activities that focused on shared activities with him, e.g., going on walks, sunbathing, and running errands. These provided unexpected pleasures that interrupted the pattern of pain in her life. During this time she became acquainted with other dog owners and went on weekly outings with them, as they took their dogs to the park. People would comment on what a wonderful dog she had, and she would begin to talk with them about him. She brought him once to a therapy session and frequently brought pictures of their outings and told anecdotes of his antics. She became more animated in her self-expression and was able to laugh more fluidly, both at herself and her dog. Her curiosity had now truly enticed her far afield from her rigidly narrow and quite predictable patterns of suicidal ideation. She was able to engage in a wider variety of healthy, pleasurable risk-taking behaviors. She spoke to more people on a variety of everyday topics, began joining local groups that were not recovery related, and took a greater interest in her appearance and physical surroundings.

Despite the loss of employment, improvements were seen in a variety of areas. She could now accept how limited her life had become as a result of her abusive history. In small ways, she began to venture out by establishing interpersonal relationships beyond therapy. She also began taking an interest in the food she ate. For more than five years she had demonstrated no variation in her evening meal. She would prepare a large quantity of tuna noodle casserole every Sunday. She then ate only that for her evening meal until the next Sunday, when the cycle was repeated. Now she found herself able to try other types of food and began experimenting with combinations of foods and recipes. She began seeing more clearly how continuing to focus exclusively on her memories of past abuse impeded her living in the present. Her view of herself and what being an adult was all about shifted from an avoidance of responsibility to a willingness to see herself as capable of creating her own life. Sparking her curiosity aided her in breaking through these learned limitations and allowed her to make more creative choices throughout the spectrum of her life.

Case Two

Sexual dysfunction is frequently seen among the presenting problems of incest and sexual abuse survivors. An inability to tolerate tactile sensations appears to be part of this dysfunction. Maltz and Holman, in *Incest and Sexuality: A Guide to Understanding and Healing* (1987), state:

> Lack of sexual desire is a common complaint of incest survivors. It appears related to an array of problems associated with arousal. Regardless of whether survivors felt pain, pleasure or numbness during the actual physical experience of the incest, most of them seem to identify sexual arousal with feelings they were having during the abuse. At the time of the incest, their concept of sexuality and their biological response to sexual stimulation became associated with their negative feelings toward the abuse. Consequently, if survivors felt helplessness, anger or guilt at the time of the abuse, they may later

find these same feelings surfacing as soon as they begin to engage in sexual behavior. (pp. 75–76)

Curiosity is a natural part of childhood exploration of sexuality. For the incest/sexual abuse survivor, that curiosity is thwarted by the premature exposure to adult sexuality. The mixed feelings of pleasure and shame, which come at the expense of self-worth, inhibit the child from venturing out to explore sensations and experiences in a healthy way.

Sarah, a 28-year-old married woman, presented for therapy with the complaint of painful intercourse. She had been in treatment previously with little or no success in reducing her pain. She was chronically depressed and had been participating in a variety of 12-step programs for incest survivors and those addicted to alcohol and food. She had difficulty maintaining emotional boundaries in her relationships and had torturous guilt if she did not reveal everything when asked direct questions.

She initially perceived the sexual dysfunction as psychological but then decided it was medically based when a physician was willing to pursue exploratory surgery. Mild endometriosis was found, and the tissue was removed successfully. To her dismay, symptoms continued. She continued to consult other physicians in the hope of finding medical explanations for her problems.

Treatment during this time focused on the three components of pain: the anticipation of pain, the emotional response to pain, and the physical pain itself. Repeated discussions were held about the nature and relative extent of these components. Sarah was encouraged to think of these components as thirds that had vaguely mutual boundaries. This allowed her to begin looking at her pain with more curiosity. Could she define what 45 percent anticipated pain might represent in terms of sensations and experience? Was her emotional response to pain able to move from 33 to 25 percent and how would she know when her response had decreased? Could the portion of her perceived pain that was actually physical be changed so that its 33 percent no longer represented one-third of her perceived pain? During the course of treatment, she further reported having numerous phobias. Several concerned taking baths. In contrast, she stated that she felt comfortable in a swimming pool with her husband. She was instructed to go skinny dipping in her swimming pool, which she found an intriguing idea. She was also instructed to stand in her bathtub clad in a bathing suit with only a few inches of water to cover her feet. While in the bathtub, she was to take a handful of pennies and see how many different ways she could toss the coins into the water to make a wish.

Still focused on her need for a medical explanation for her painful intercourse, she found another physician who would perform the same exploratory surgery. She was given total permission to seek out as many answers in as many different ways as she needed. However, because of her tendency toward defensive oppositionality, it was suggested to her in therapy that perhaps she just did not want to have sex with her husband. She became angry at this suggestion. Over the course of the next week, she had sex with him several times, reporting later that it was less painful. One of her physicians stated that an allergy might be causing her pain, which she described as a "vaginal sore throat." It was suggested in therapy that allergies sometimes arise from using something too frequently. Because she had never questioned the interactive effect of lubricants on her sexual experiences, she was encouraged to see how many different lubricants she could find on the market. She became intrigued with comparing the ingredients of her current lubricant to those of others on the market, with the idea of finding one with different ingredients that might feel different and work in a different way. At the same time she was challenged in therapy to discover exactly how many different ways there are to engage in sexual behavior. She turned on lights in the bedroom, because her father had abused her in the dark. She began making noises during intercourse, because, as a child, she had been extremely quiet and fearful during her abuse. She also experimented with having sex in different locations in the house and even in the swimming pool. By using her curiosity about different ways of controlling her environment and her responses to sexual experiences, she was able to eliminate the pain that she experienced in intercourse and to increase her sense of pleasure, excitement, and safety.

Conclusion

Reestablishing natural curiosity within the patient aided her in taking her future development into her own hands. It fostered a self-confidence in learning and changing that opened doors and broadened the range of future outcomes. Incest and sexual abuse survivors have been robbed of this enriched way of learning. Ericksonian learning approaches allow the therapist's own curiosity and interest in life to be brought directly into the therapeutic relationship as a primary agent of change, moving the individual toward healthier, more pleasure-oriented living. No other philosophy, therapeutic technique, or personality theory has offered therapists such a cornucopia of valuable tools for assisting people to stimulate, discover, and revive their own unconscious resources for creative adaptation to life. Erickson's masterly use and enjoyment of his own and other's curiosity was one of his most important yet least described contributions to the mental health field.

References

Courtois, A. (1988). *Healing the incest wound: Adult survivors in therapy.* New York: Norton.

Erickson, M. H., Rossi, E., Ryan, M. O., & Sharp, F. A. (Eds.). (1985). *Healing in hypnosis (Vol. 1): The seminars, workshops, and lectures of Milton H. Erickson.* New York: Irvington.

Erickson, M. H. (1985). Redirecting the subject's attention. In E. Rossi & M. O. Ryan (Eds.), *Life reframing in hypnosis (Vol. 2): The seminars, workshops, and lectures of Milton H. Erickson* (pp. 146–148). New York: Irvington.

Erickson, M. H., & Rossi, E. (1979). *Hypnotherapy: An Exploratory Casebook.* New York: Irvington.

Erickson, M. H., & Rossi, E. (Eds.). (1985). *Mind-body communication in hypnosis (Vol. 3): The seminars, workshops, and lectures of Milton H. Erickson.* New York: Irvington.

Erickson, M. H., & Rossi, E. (Eds.). (1989). *The collected papers of Milton H. Erickson on hypnosis (Vol. 1): The nature of hypnosis and suggestion.* New York: Irvington.

Erickson, M. H., & Rossi, E. (Eds.). (1989a). *The collected papers of Milton H. Erickson on hypnosis (Vol. 2): Hypnotic alteration of sensory, perceptual and psychophysiological processes.* New York: Irvington.

Erickson, M. H., & Rossi, E. (Eds.). (1989b). *The collected papers of Milton H. Erickson on hypnosis (Vol. 3): Hypnotic investigation of psychodynamic processes.* New York: Irvington.

Erickson, M. H., & Rossi, E. (Eds.). (1989c). *The collected papers of Milton H. Erickson on hypnosis (Vol. 4): Innovative hypnotherapy.* New York: Irvington Press.

Maltz, W., & Holman, B. (1987). *Incest and sexuality: A guide to understanding and healing.* Lexington, MA: Lexington Books.

Rosen, S. (1982). *My voice will go with you: The teaching tales of Milton H. Erickson.* New York: Norton.

Russell, D. E. (1986). *The secret trauma: Incest in the lives of girls and women.* New York: Basic Books.

Van der Kolk, A. (1987). *Psychological trauma.* Washington, DC: American Psychiatric Press.

Personality Restructuring from an Ericksonian Perspective

Don Malon, Ph.D., and Wendy Hurley, M.A.

Personality restructuring meant, for Erickson, reassociating and reorganizing the patient's phenomenal world. With some patients Erickson did uncovering work that resembled traditional psychotherapy. However, he was unique in his use of hypnotic amnesia and in his management of a clearly delineated separation between conscious and unconscious awareness. We describe an approach to personality restructuring that more gradually aligns and integrates conscious and unconscious division. We describe and illustrate five ways in which Erickson influenced and shaped our approach: (a) viewing neurotic responses as obstacles to development; (b) minimizing interpretation while maximizing experience; (c) facilitating the "inner articulation" process; (d) utilizing transference and resistance; and (e) emphasizing the two-person relationship.

When years ago Jay Haley (1985) asked Milton Erickson whether he did personality restructuring, Erickson answered yes, with the following qualification: "[Patients] can accept those neurotic manifestations as not purely a defect in themselves but a response in themselves. Therefore, if they can make a wrong response, they can learn a good response" (p. 102). He then mentioned the case of a man he sent on a date, who, on suddenly becoming nauseated at the woman's homely appearance, associated his reaction to memories of his mother's snobbishness. Erickson avoided use of interpretation here, realizing long ago what modern analysts such as Kenneth Wright (1991) are seeing today: that in interpreting and analyzing, one holds a client's experience at a distance, one abstract step removed from the more immediate and tangible process of "inner articulation" (Wright, 1991, p. 293). Wright clarifies this process by referring to

Address correspondence to Don Malon, Ph.D., School of Social Service, St. Louis University, 3550 Lindell Blvd., St. Louis, MO 63103.

Winnicott's statement that it is the "felt joining together of things" that has to precede insight.

In Erickson's case, the man supplied his own insight, gained as an outcome of both outer and inner articulations—that is, he took action in dating the woman, which led to his feeling-awareness. Also, he was permitted to view his "neurotic response" not as a defect to be analyzed but as an opportunity to learn a new autonomous response. In *February Man* (Erickson & Rossi, 1989), Rossi captures the essence of Erickson's approach in saying to him, "You don't just analyze and understand; rather you evoke and utilize the mental processes within the person" (pp. 148–149).

Rossi was discovering here that a unique aspect of Erickson's work was in evoking and utilizing mental processes. However, this work was not to avoid insight; rather, it often served as a means by which patients gained their own insight. For Erickson, as for Freud, the unconscious as the source of developmental blocks could be made conscious in some fashion. Erickson states this explicitly in some of his work, and only implicitly at other times. Erickson (1977) said, "One tries to do hypnotherapy at an unconscious level but to give the patient an opportunity to transfer that understanding and insight to the conscious mind as far as it is needed" (p. 21).

"As far as it is needed" is an elusive phrase. Clearly, there are examples of Erickson's work in which patients do not appear to have needed any understanding of why they changed. We will be concerned here with the others, because we believe they illustrate more clearly the importance that Erickson placed on personality restructuring.

It has been pointed out by others (Haley, 1986; Rossi, Ryan, and Sharp, 1983) that Erickson's understanding of developmental processes played a large part in his work. However, for Erickson, personality restructuring did not refer to the overhaul of one's infantile memories and the exclusive reliance on the remote past. Instead, personality restructuring meant the "reassociation and reorganization of ideas, understandings, and memories" (Erickson, 1980c, p. 38)—that is, the restructuring of the patient's phenomenal world. As Erickson (1980c) said, "It is the experience of reassociating and reorganizing his own experiential life that eventuates in a cure" (p. 38). He even went so far as to disparage symptomatic cure because it did not entail this inner reorganization. Zeig and Geary (1990, p. 108) recognized this stance when they pointed out that even in his direct, action-oriented work with symptoms, Erickson aimed for a "snowballing therapeutic reorganization" that would show itself in the patient's relationships, including the relationships within the patient.

There was a place for insight and understanding in Erickson's work, and he did recognize in some form that the unconscious may need to be translated into consciousness. Also, Erickson could deal with past as well as present life experience in order to bring about a personality reorganization that led to growth and development. It is easier to recognize these processes in those cases in which he dealt directly with the past, such as the instance in which Erickson had patients relive early trauma through catharsis and abreaction (Haley, 1986). Even here, however, Erickson's focus was unique. Instead of proceeding as most depth therapists do, from the conscious level to the unconscious level, he typically reversed the process, starting at the unconscious level. He would do this by inducing hypnotic amnesia, thereby preventing the conscious mind from interfering with unconscious processing. In doing so, he pointed out that it was an error not to recognize the separateness of conscious and unconscious levels of awareness. Erickson (1980c) also recognized that it was a goal of therapy to bring about integration of conscious and unconscious awareness—in his words, "the integration of the total personality" (p. 40).

It takes great mastery to induce a somnambulistic trance, employ amnesia, and create a sharp separateness between levels of awareness, while eventually achieving conscious–unconscious integration. As Erickson (1980b) said, "Hypnosis is often the royal road to memories, although it still leaves the task of integrating that memory into the waking life of the patient a painstaking task for the therapist" (p. 20). Even though in Erickson's published work he could make the task of integration appear simple, we therapists are well advised to heed his caution.

For those of us who wish to learn from Erickson, the point at issue here is how much separateness to maintain between conscious and unconscious levels. In our restructuring approach, we work with a different balance of conscious–unconscious separateness than Erickson did. As a result, we deal with smaller amounts of unconscious content. The result is a satisfactory therapeutic trade-off. Although we have less unconscious leverage to begin with, it is a less painstaking process to achieve points of integration.

With these thoughts to guide us, we would like to present five principles, derived largely from Erickson's work, which inform our approach to personality restructuring.

Viewing Neurotic Responses as Obstacles to Development

We have learned from Erickson to view a client's neurotic responses as obstacles to development rather than as psychopathology. It is noteworthy that in Rossi's (1972) first original work he used the concept "symptoms of development" to denote the often nightmarish anxiety that can occur in dreams. He took the Jungian view that anxiety contained the seeds of growth and change. Instead of interpreting the content, he helped his patient to reflect on her dreams and articulate her own meaning. He was to discover that this approach to dreams was consistent with Erickson's tendency to accept and go with, to utilize, whatever the person brings, including his or her symptoms. In our initial example, Erickson sent his patient on a date before he was cured of his neurotic anxiety, thereby utilizing the anxiety with the presumption that it contained growth potential. Indeed, the date did generate the anxiety but also the felt-meaning that helped the patient correct his problem behavior.

One of our clients, a 37-year-old man, suffered from depression and intense shame, with an undercurrent of rage and helplessness. He was already aware that his symptoms had their roots in his childhood relationship with a hysterically abusive, seductive mother. He had all the conventional insight he could handle, and it had no effect on his symptoms. He came to his fourth session feeling mortified because his bank had confronted him with an error in his checking account. In trance he expanded on this "neurotic" response and evoked a feeling of having fallen into a bottomless pit. He produced the image of a boy's blob-like chest, devoid of head, arms, and legs, feeling ready to explode. The image was frightening. Thanks to the dissociational effect of trance he could tolerate the image and could imagine holding the blob together. He learned that it represented the boy's traumatized reaction to a mother's ongoing physical abuse. After this felt-experience, with little discussion of the meaning, he reported a series of interpersonal confrontations with markedly decreased anxiety.

Minimizing Interpretation; Maximizing Experience

In the above example, interpretation is minimized. The pitfall of interpretation is that it keeps the client at the conceptual level rather than the perceptual level. Wright (1991) states it rather strongly: "Interpretation provides an escape from being overwhelmed by some feeling experience" (p. 293). An active, experiential approach is not painless, as the above cases illustrate, even though, as Gindhart (1985) says, "The promise of hypnotic psychotherapy is to produce experiential relief" (p. 113). It is our task to provide reorganizing experiences, and we need to take care to provide them, as Erickson (1977) said, "in the order in which the patient can assimilate them" (p. 20).

In experiential therapy, the issue of emotional intensity is a challenge, especially when dealing with trauma. Erickson (1980d) saw the therapeutic task here as taking a painful personal experience and "rendering it into an objective matter" (p. 394). In other words, as subjective emotional intensity increases, we help increase the amount of objective thinking. Hypnosis is a good vehicle because it permits dissociation between the process of experiencing and what Erickson (1980d, p. 393) called an "observational modality" that watches the experiencing. For the traumatized client this state involves an interesting paradox. From the hypnotic dissociated position of the observer modality, he or she is helped to reassociate and thereby reorganize painful past experiences.

For example, our client, a 40-year-old victim of incest and ritual abuse, was beginning to recall an early painful memory while in trance. To keep her at a safe distance from the emotional intensity, it was suggested she see the experience occurring in a crystal ball (Erickson, 1977, pg. 28). As the scene started to unfold, she said, "It's too close. I can't look." She was then told to put the crystal ball "up there in a corner of her mind," and she was assured that she could take her time to find just the right, safe distance that was presently necessary. She relived the experience to her satisfaction and continued to find the right balance of emotional intensity and objectivity during subsequent sessions.

Facilitating the "Inner Articulation" Process

As Erickson and Rossi (1989), pointed out, "Therapy is getting the patient to use his own processes....you can only help the person within his own phenomenal world" (pp. 149–150). Rossi (1989) termed this process the "language of human facilitation" (p. 82). It involved helping the patient discover the places where the learning stopped and then finding the inner resources to resume the growth process and resolve the problem. The inner articulation alluded to by Erickson and Rossi involves some degree of awareness. However, it neither means passive, insight-seeking awareness nor does it involve suggestion. It means active cognitive and emotional work. As Erickson and Rossi (1989) put it, "A patient has to do hard work, active work in trance" (p. 242).

We agree with Beahrs (1977), who adds a feeling dimension to the articulation process. He observed that one of the "approaches" Erickson employed was the "awareness approach," which entailed dealing with inner feeling states. Beahrs realized that his observation would be seen as controversial, so he asked Erickson to comment on it. Erickson conceded that Beahrs was on target. We believe that Beahrs's focus on feeling awareness is consistent with Erickson's work because such a focus is a means of eliciting unconscious dynamics. It is a way to let the unconscious "take primacy" (Beahrs, 1977, p. 63). Wright (1991) clarifies the connection between feelings and the unconscious when he says, "Consciousness is the attitude of trying to know my feeling self with words" (p. 154). Feelings about one's self, especially "primary feelings" (Greenberg & Safran, 1987, p. 172), are rooted in our earliest learnings. Conscious verbal articulation is not sufficient to evoke them and break through the learning impasses preventing growth. An experiential focus on feeling awareness can break the unconscious barrier.

Watkins's "affect bridge" technique (1971) is an excellent example of how to access unconscious feelings rooted in the past by focusing on a current feeling state. He simply directs the patient in trance to focus explicitly on symptomatic feelings and sensations and to imagine that they could be a bridge to some earlier feelings and experiences existing at the unconscious level. Erickson was not reluctant to focus directly on feeling awareness. In one case Erickson (1980a) asked his patient, Edward C., to have a series of hypnotic dreams in order to understand the reasons he was in a mental hospital. With Erickson holding his hand for comfort, the patient underwent four emotionally wrenching dreams during four sessions. They culminated in Edward's awareness of his suicidal feelings stemming from his parents' shameful abuse and his newfound hatred for what they did to him.

Utilizing Transference and Resistance

Transference and resistance go hand in hand. In traditional forms of therapy, resistance is confronted by analyzing and interpreting transference reactions. Erickson took a different view, a very humane and respectful view. He simply considered people's resistant behaviors as their best effort at cooperating while getting their personal and interpersonal needs met (Lankton, 1985). Similarly, regarding transference, Erickson (Haley, 1985) said, "Sure the patients develop a tremendous transference, but that isn't what's wrong with them. That's their method of getting rid of what's wrong with them" (p. 90).

Erickson's acceptance of transference and resistance as normal did not mean that they were to be ignored. In fact, he paid close attention to these behaviors and was ready to make use of them as he would make use of any of the patient's behaviors. He saw transference as "a bridge" (Haley, 1985, p. 90) to be made use of as a means for getting to something more important that the patient had been avoiding. In working with a stutterer, Erickson (1977) saw repressed anger as the key dynamic, and because the patient transferred that anger to his therapist, Erickson simply encouraged the transference. After the therapy had succeeded the patient said to Erickson (1977), "You gave me a certain hatred that was very, very useful, and my psychoanalyst tried to take it away from me" (p. 33). This patient had been avoiding the expression of his anger, and so the stuttering. The experience of anger proved more curative than the interpretation of it.

Treating transference as a bridge requires that we accept and go along with the resistance involved, utilizing it in some here-and-now, experiential way in order to get past it to some more important dynamic. Actually, Erickson would not wait for resistance and transference dynamics to present themselves. In keeping with his active, experiential approach, his first rule of therapy was to get the patient to do something, whether that be climbing a mountain or going out on a date. We suggest that it is getting the client to do something different that can make the difference. Stirring something up outside the client can activate responses inside that can aid the reorganizing process.

In the following case illustration, a resistant pattern was revealed and an active intervention arranged. This intervention evoked a transference response that resulted in a change in the client. Dr. B. was a middle-aged, compulsively active dentist who had a history of clinging to women for sex and security. He was aware of an undercurrent of deep sadness and of the fact that having sex with women made him feel alive. He had been born one-and-a-half years after the death of a 12-year-old brother and consequently became the son who carried the brunt of his parents' unresolved grief and fear.

Dr. B. kept himself so busy that he rarely had an idle moment. He called this part of himself "Mr. Doer." Recognizing this as an avoidant, resistant pattern of behavior, the therapist persuaded Dr. B. to take a break from Mr. Doer by staying in bed for an hour or so in the morning and introspecting with quiet curiosity. Dr. B. did surprisingly well, staying in bed on three occasions during the week, tolerating the inactivity and reflecting on the women in his life. As he reported to his therapist, "I noticed I went back through all my relationships, starting in junior high school, and I wasn't aware I was doing it, but I noticed any time I was in a relationship with any woman there was always another one in the background."

After a week of successfully confronting Mr. Doer, while riding his bike to the next session, Dr. B. suddenly found his heart racing and felt an apprehension that he had failed to do enough to please his therapist. In the session he cried while telling her this. The therapist asked him to go inside and track the feeling associated with his transference response back to an earlier source. The result was his discovery that he had a lifelong fear of being judged and graded about doing the right thing. In addition, he realized a continual fear of physical harm, which was associated with his parents' overprotection. To complete the train of associations, he felt terrible remorse about his clinging and rejecting treatment of women. He concluded tearfully, "I'm seeing women differently than I ever have before. God, it's releasing!"

Emphasizing the Two-Person Relationship

Erickson believed that "therapists should be oriented to their patients instead of their theories" (Gindhart, 1985, p. 114). In other words, our theories can keep us from seeing the distinctness and uniqueness of the individual. By implication, we need a theory that encourages us to face the full complexity of the person. To achieve the goal of reassociating and reorganizing the patient's experience, we must, as Gindhart (1985) says, do so "in accord with the distinct experiential history and the unique requirements of every individual" (p. 131).

Some observations by Wright (1991) may clarify this issue. Wright (1991, p. 312) makes a distinction between a "two-person" relationship and a "three-person" relationship. The two-person relationship is a self-to-self relationship wherein the therapist uses his or her own self to reflect and resonate with the patient as a self, not as an object. Erickson would refer to this as the unconscious-to-unconscious communication that trance provides. In the three-person position, the therapist becomes observer and conceptualizer. Thus, the intimate contact of the two-person relationship is the database for the three-person relationship. The three-person position is for Erickson none other than the "objective modality," wherein therapist and patient come to understand the meaning expressed in the patient's experiencing. Being oriented to our patients instead of our theories means knowing how to get close enough to our patients to enable them to get close enough to themselves to do reorganizing work.

With Dr. B., the therapist made the two-person relationship primary, keeping the three-person position secondary, Dr. B.'s objective understanding about his past "wrong" behavior was not what changed him. What was primary was the experiential relationship context which evoked what Erickson (1980c) referred to as a "train of mental activity." That train of mental activity resulted in Dr. B.'s reorganizing his feelings and attitudes about women. Yet he could not understand why he still felt sad, lonely feelings. In a later session the therapist drew Dr. B.'s attention to his habit of sitting with his feet constantly moving. She asked him to close his eyes and notice what it was like not to move his feet. After a pause he said, "I feel dead." He choked up and cried, recalling lying on his back as an infant, feeling the crib bar and being aware that nobody was coming. He would kick his feet to feel alive. This new train of associations was initiated in the two-person relationship. The empathic, mutual curiosity of therapist and client resulted in the client's getting closer to himself so that he could have an emotionally corrective experience. This case is also an example of how self-disclosure about the past can serve our ultimate goal, which was for Erickson (Haley, 1967) "the present and future adjustment of the patient" (p. 406).

Summary and Conclusions

We have tried to show that Erickson's psychotherapy entailed personality restructuring, that is, restructuring of the patient's phenomenal world through reassociation and reorganization of the patient's ideas, understandings, and memories. For Erickson, as for more traditional therapists, memories could involve repressed material, leading to insight or new understandings. However, Erickson was unique in the way he structured this part of therapy. Although he aimed to integrate new unconscious understandings with conscious awareness, he did this the hard way by starting with a sharp separation between conscious and unconscious levels of awareness and by employing amnesia to prevent conscious interference with unconscious processing. We say "the hard way" because not only does it require great skill to manage this degree of conscious/unconscious division, but, we believe, it makes integration with consciousness a more difficult task for the therapist. For those clients with whom we do uncovering work leading to personality reorganization, we have indicated our one point of departure from Erickson's work with similar patients, that is, our preference for dealing with smaller pieces of unconscious material and for a gradual, incremental integration with consciousness.

Our approach is otherwise consistent with Erickson's and indeed very much influenced by him. We described five specific influences that provide a foundation for our work. First, we view neurotic responses as obstacles to development. We believe, as does Erickson, that a so-called neurotic response is nothing more than a wrong response that has not yet been corrected. The strength of neurotic responses should not diminish our hopefulness about the client's capacity for new learning. Second, we posited that interpretation should be minimized and experience maximized. Hypnotherapy can produce insight, but it is the client's insight that is important, not the therapist's. Furthermore, insight will be productive and useful to the extent it arises from new experiencing, whether inside or outside the therapy sessions.

To describe a third influence, we referred to Wright's (1991) principle of facilitating the inner articulation process. We do not just probe and explore the client's phenomenal world. We facilitate a process of active cognitive and emotional work under trance conditions. We have highlighted the notion of feeling-awareness because of the capability of feelings to evoke unconscious dynamics. A fourth influence involves the utilizing of transference and resistance. Transference responses are to be respected, at times even encouraged, and at other times viewed as a bridge to something more important. In experiential therapy the client can enact transference and resistance, not to provide grist for interpretation but, rather, as the basis for corrective experience. Our last influence is the two-person relationship, and our emphasis on it. The distinction between a two-person relationship and a three-person relationship marks the difference between a relationship that is truly experiential and one that is conceptual and objective. We try to show that there is a place for both orientations. However, we believe the three-person position is best represented by Erickson's concept of the objective modality, that is, that safe objective distance from the experiencing, where meaning and understanding take place. Thus, it is not the therapist who is to interpret and conceive the meaning of the client's experience; rather, it is the meaning as perceived by the client that is valued in this approach.

Personality restructuring can connote an exhaustive, time-consuming process, as it has tended to be in traditional forms of therapy. This is not the case with an Ericksonian perspective. In fact, experiential hypnotherapy that is oriented to significant growth and development is a very focused, purposefully engaging therapy. In describing how hypnotherapy directs attention to the potentialities within the person, Erickson (1980a) drew a precise analogy. He said, "This is as important as the conventional scientific laboratory, because it is the laboratory that exists within the person" (p. 58). The cure that emanates from this laboratory leads to the reorganization of one's experiential life.

References

Beahrs, J. O. (1977). Integrating Erickson's approach. *American Journal of Clinical Hypnosis, 20*, 55–68.

Erickson, M. H. (1977). Hypnotic approaches to therapy. *American Journal of Clinical Hypnosis, 20*, 20–35.

Erickson, M. H. (1980a). Hypnosis: Its renascence as a treatment modality. In E. L. Rossi (Ed.), *The collected papers of Milton H. Erickson on hypnosis: Vol. 4. Innovative hypnotherapy* (pp. 52–75). New York: Irvington.

Erickson, M.H. (1980b). Hypnosis in medicine. In E. L. Rossi (Ed.), *The collected papers of Milton H. Erickson on hypnosis: Vol. 4. Innovative hypnotherapy* (pp. 14–27). New York: Irvington.

Erickson, M. H. (1980c). Hypnotic psychotherapy. In E. L. Rossi (Ed.), *The collected papers of Milton H. Erickson on hypnosis: Vol. 4. Innovative hypnotherapy* (pp. 35–48). New York: Irvington.

Erickson, M. H. (1980d). Self-exploration in the hypnotic state: Facilitating unconscious processes and objective thinking. In E. L. Rossi (Ed.), *The collected papers of Milton H. Erickson on hypnosis: Vol. 4. Innovative hypnotherapy* (pp. 393–396). New York: Irvington.

Erickson, M. H. & Rossi, E. L. (1989). *The February man: Evolving consciousness and identity in hypnotherapy.* New York: Irvington.

Gindhart, L. R. (1985). Hypnotic psychotherapy. In J. K. Zeig (Ed.), *Ericksonian psychotherapy: Vol. 1. Structures* (pp. 110–134). New York: Brunner/Mazel.

Greenberg, L. S., and Safran, J. D. (1987). *Emotion in psychotherapy: Affect, cognition, and the process of change.* New York: Guilford.

Haley, J. (Ed.). (1967). *Advanced techniques of hypnosis and therapy: Selected papers of Milton H. Erickson, M.D.* New York: Grune & Stratton.

Haley, J. (1985). *Conversations with Milton H. Erickson, M.D.: Vol. 1. Changing individuals.* New York: Triangle Press.

Haley, J. (1986). *Uncommon therapy: The psychiatric techniques of Milton H. Erickson, M.D.* New York: Norton.

Lankton, S. R. (1985). A states of consciousness model of Ericksonian hypnosis. In S. R. Lankton (Ed.), *Ericksonian monographs, No. 1: Elements and dimensions of an Ericksonian approach* (pp. 26–41). New York: Brunner/Mazel.

Rossi, E. L. (1972). *Dreams and the growth of personality: Expanding awareness in psychotherapy.* New York: Pergamon.

Rossi, E. L. (1989). Facilitating "creative moments" in hypnotherapy. In S. R. Lankton and J. K. Zeig (Eds.), *Ericksonian monographs, No. 6: Extrapolations: Demonstrations of Ericksonian therapy* (pp. 81–99). New York: Brunner/Mazel.

Rossi, E. L., Ryan, M. O., & Sharp, F. A. (Eds.). (1983). *Healing in hypnosis: The seminars, workshops, and lectures of Milton H. Erickson.* New York: Irvington.

Watkins, J. G. (1971). The affect bridge: A hypnoanalytic technique. *International Journal of Clinical and Experimental Hypnosis, 19,* 21–27.

Wright, K. (1991). *Vision and separation between mother and baby.* Northvale, NJ: Jason Aronson.

Zeig, J. K., & Geary, B. B. (1990). Seeds of strategic and interactional psychotherapies: Seminal contributions of Milton H. Erickson. *American Journal of Clinical Hypnosis, 33,* 105–112.

Symbolic Therapy: Two Cases of Refusal to Attend School

Keiichi Miyata, M.A.

Two patients were treated with solution-focused symbolic therapy. Through hypnosis, a 15-year-old boy's interpersonal fear and his concern about his hair were displaced to a weak part of his mind and located symbolically in his body in a form of imagery. His confident part was induced, and it was suggested that he integrate both parts. He spontaneously generated a new symbol that made him active. Another patient was treated without hypnosis. A teased 10-year-old girl's anxiety of being isolated in her class was solved through a symbol-making activity. Both therapeutic processes can be seen as the transformation ones of the clients' stories. It is suggested that the clients' positive coping sets as the agents of the solution were a necessary part of the therapy.

Erickson treated emotional problems with a variety of techniques in which the utilization of symbols or symbolic acts was central. In the treatment of a patient for an "airplane phobia" (Erickson & Rossi, 1979; Zeig, 1980), Erickson displaced her fears onto a chair she was sitting on and had pictures of the chair taken. The patient took the pictures as her good luck charm on an airplane trip. The pictures were the externalized symbols of her fears through which she could be freed from them. The containment of her fears gave her relief, and the symbols could be "protection" against her fears. The pictures were multidimensional, and symbolized both her confined fears and her protection. Symbolizing a symptom or problem externally can be called *problem-oriented symbolic therapy*.

In another case, one of a depressed mother who had lost her baby (Zeig, 1980), Erickson suggested she plant a eucalyptus sapling and name it Cynthia, her baby's name. The tree was considered a new symbol that

Address correspondence to Keiichi Miyata, M.A., Faculty of Education, Niigata University, 8050, Ikarashi Ni-No-Cho, Niigata-Shi, Japan 950-21.

represented both her separation from the depression and the beginning a new life. The client's depressive feeling was absorbed by the tree, and she could look forward to tending it as it grew. In this case Erickson used a technique of providing a new symbol, one that was oriented to a positive aspect of the client and her future. This method can be called *solution-oriented symbolic therapy*, which is different from problem-oriented symbolic therapy. In this chapter, solution-oriented symbolic therapy is emphasized. Two clients are presented for illustration.

Case One

A 15-year-old boy was brought to our guidance clinic center by his mother. She complained that the boy had refused to go to school for about two years because of his concern about his hair. The boy had suffered from interpersonal fear and avoided interpersonal contact (even answering the phone) ever since he was teased about his hair in school. He believed his hair was thin at the front. A dermatologist had found no abnormalities. The mother had suffered from diabetes for more than 10 years. The boy also suffered from mild diabetes and had taken medication since he was in the fifth grade, when he began to hate going to school.

The boy's parents had divorced when he was four years old. His father had had an affair and abused his mother physically during their marriage. After the divorce, the boy and his mother began living with the maternal grandmother. The mother worked as a hostess at a bar at night and had a boyfriend whom the boy hated. The mother forced him to go to school, and the boy became violent toward her and the grandmother. The grandmother separated from the family and was living alone by the time the boy entered junior high school. From then on, the boy lived with his mother. When he was in junior high school, the mother began to allow him to stay away from school, and his violence toward her disappeared.

The boy reported to the interview room wearing a cap and sat turned away from the therapist because of his interpersonal anxiety. He spoke haltingly, and walked bowlegged with his head down.

He spoke of being interested in science fiction novels and religion. He was influenced by a book called *Great Prophecies from the Spiritual World* and believed that a new ice age would come in 1999 and ordinary people would die; the elite would be saved by spacemen. He despaired of his future and said the inferior level of humanity, of which he was a part, would not be taken to another planet.

Eighteen therapeutic sessions with seven hypnotic interviews were conducted. In the hypnotic sessions, before reorienting the client, amnesia was suggested to protect him. At first the therapist worked to form a therapeutic relationship with the boy and, utilizing the boy's habit of reading the newspaper every day, suggested that he make some comments on a newspaper article. He had a word processor and spontaneously began to type his comments. In the third session the therapist induced hypnosis for the first time, using hand levitation, as an exercise to relax the boy. In the fifth session, under hypnosis, the boy's anxiety about his hair was displaced to a weak part of his mind and was located in his body symbolically as a form of imagery, along with a confident part. He said that each part consisted of a layer expanding all over his body. When the therapist asked him if white corpuscles were there to protect his body, his response was positive. After waking, he was asked to type the pros and cons as well as his integrative comments on newspaper articles from then on. The themes he described were almost always about social and political problems, including environmental pollution, population, and war.

In the next session the therapist worked to have the strong and weak parts coexist and suggested that the weak part would be located within the confident part. The weak part was located symbolically in the boy's heart, where two magicians, male and female, dwelled. They were about 20 years old, with black mantles covering their bodies, and were standing in a place like a meadow. The boy wanted to expel them from his heart. After the therapist suggested that he open his eyes, draw the scene and close his eyes again, the suggestion of covering his heart was given. The boy said that although he tried it, the cover was broken and the magicians reappeared. He could not complete the covering until the therapist got assistance from his white corpuscles.

In the seventh session the therapist asked the mother about her boyfriend. She said she had started seeing her boyfriend 18 months after her divorce. The boy called her boyfriend "Uncle" and was taken to the playground by him. Recently the boy had seemed to begin to hate her boyfriend.

In the next session, under hypnosis, the boy imaged a red part in his body as his weak part. The confident part was green and surrounded the weak one. (In the fifth session, the green part had been represented as the weak one.) While the boy was visualizing, he moved his left hand (he was left-handed) to his right shoulder and acted as if he were massaging it because of his bodily tension. During this time the red part was expanding in his imagery. The therapist moved the boy's right hand to his left shoulder and the therapist put his own hand on the boy's right shoulder, suggesting his right shoulder felt warm and relaxed, and his left shoulder felt rather tense. In addition, the therapist suggested the balance of the two parts change. Consequently, the boy felt both shoulders relax. The boy felt the red part was a little bit larger than the green part and said there seemed to be something that could break up the red part. In this session, the boy brought his written daily schedule, an assignment given to him previously, and he had also started studying at home for three hours a day.

In the ninth session, under hypnosis, the boy imaged space expanding and saw shining orange stars and darkness, of which he felt frightened. The boy then saw a flying saucer, which made him relieved, and he saw a box being dropped from the flying saucer. He felt it was regretable to throw the box away because it was valuable. In this session, he also brought comments (as was his task) in which he predicted a change, quoting the remarks of a female spiritualist: A group of spirits led by Yukio Mishima (a Japanese novelist) would come to Japan in a UFO to start a revolution, and the prophecy would be shown to be true or false on the next January 7.

At the end of the session, he was given a task of walking straight with his head up, and his behavior changed positively. He had his hair cut by a barber for the first time since his school refusal started. He said that he would like to start a high school correspondence course. He changed his attitude toward his mother's conduct with her boyfriend and did not object to whatever his mother did outside his sight. He started building new relationships through correspondence. He said he had written a letter unconsciously to the editors of a magazine, and he had forgotten about it until he got a response.

In the thirteenth session he came to therapy alone for the first time. He was happy and reported that he believed he had seen a shooting star or a UFO after midnight on January 7, although he did not identify it exactly. He said, "I would like to believe it was a UFO." Hypnotic imagery was induced, and he was asked how the balance of his mind was. He saw a tiny yellow area in the darkness. The therapist suggested the light change his living style and his future, and as his distress and suffering were absorbed into the yellow light, his confidence would be bolstered and the color would become brighter. During the session he disclosed that he had answered a call from one of his correspondents. In the fifteenth session he said, "I changed since I saw the star." He began the high school correspondence course and went to school twice a month, while he worked part time delivering newspapers early in the morning.

Case Two

This patient was treated without hypnosis. The client was a 10-year-old girl who, in addition to refusing to attend school because of teasing, suffered from psychosomatic symptoms. Her eyes dulled and her skin itched when she started talking about school. She had suffered allergic dermatitis, rhinitis, and asthma since infancy, and she was taking medication. The girl had transferred schools about seven months before her family moved, because she was ignored by her classmates. However, in this new school, she was almost forced to eat leftovers at lunch by four classmates. Her grades were good and she wanted to go to school, but she was frightened of being isolated in her class. She was an only child and stayed home during the daytime with her mother, toward whom she showed anger. While at home she liked to draw pictures or comics and make handicrafts.

The girl wanted a second transfer because of the school problem, but her parents were anxious about the possibilities that she would again be isolated or things would be worse. After the first session, the family moved to their new house, where the girl could raise a puppy named "Po Po." In the third session a behavior sequence within the family was confirmed: the girl became irritated easily and her mother reacted to it, and they then often fought. When the therapist asked for exceptions (de Shazer, 1988), the mother said the girl was calm whenever she was with her puppy. The therapist suggested that when the girl became irritated, her mother address her as "Po Po," and when the parents became angry, the girl address them as "Center" (the clinic center). The girl and her mother accepted the suggestion with hearty laughs.

In the fifth session they reported about their work with the previous task. The mother had scolded her daughter severely once, because the girl had asked her mother to wash a skirt of hers that had some tissue paper left in the pocket. The mother said, "You are teased because you never do as you are told even though I advise you many times." The girl talked back with anger, saying that the mother went too far, at which time the mother addressed the girl as "Po Po." The girl started smiling and called the mother "Center." The family also celebrated the completion of their new house with their relatives, which the therapist had suggested implicitly.

In the sixth session the mother said the attitude of the parents toward their daughter had changed positively: The father listened to his daughter patiently, and she was scolded less. Finally, despite their great concern the family decided to have the girl transfer schools again because she refused to see the four classmates again under any circumstance. When the permission for the transfer was given, the mother and daughter could not help feeling rather depressed. The girl described her feelings about the transfer as almost hopeless. The therapist suggested the girl make an embroidery or a mascot doll of "Po Po" and take it to school with her in case she became irritated or felt lonely. Some day she might forget about her mascot and make a friend. The therapist also suggested the family celebrate the transfer.

The day after the previous session, the girl began to embroider the face of her dog on a handkerchief. This took two days. The embroidered dog was praised by the father, as it was easily identified as Po Po. She also drew a picture of the dog on a card. The girl transferred schools at the second semester and started to go to school with the handkerchief and the card inside her bag. The girl said she thought of the puppy as her younger brother. The family celebrated the transfer with only moderate delight, because they had expressed great delight at the girl's first transfer, which had failed. The girl said she had become stable since she started going to her new school, and became confident.

More than one month after the girl started at her new school, her mother brought the handkerchief and the card to show to the therapist. The therapist had asked her to do so to confirm that the girl would actually attend school one day without taking them with her. The mother said the girl continued to go to school and had a new friend. She also said she could now conceive the school situation as rather positive, because the girl had been defiant to her for the first time since the school problem had begun and she had been able to keep an adequate distance from her daughter.

Transformation of the Story

As Sluzki (1992) pointed out, therapy can be viewed as a transformation of a client's story. In both cases presented here, the common problems, which were expressed in a form of school attendance refusal, were interpersonal anxiety or fear of being teased. The patients also had described themselves as victims in their personal history.

In the first case, the boy had been teased since he was in fifth grade, and he constructed the story that his hair was thin when he entered junior high school. According to Raush's model (Sluzki, 1992) of locations of problem and agency, in his story, his problem was defined as internal and the source of the solution was also depicted as internal. He felt a sense of guilt and hopelessness about the future, and came to therapy. In this case, the therapist utilized hypnotic imagery to have the client transform his old story. When the boy's concern about his hair was accepted and displaced to a weak part of his mind and was located in his body symbolically as a form of imagery, he became able to externalize his problem. Concurrently, his confident part was induced and also externalized to integrate parts. Imagery therapy has an advantage in that a client as the agent can cope with a problem that was objectified with the therapist's help. The boy spontaneously generated a new symbol that gave him more confidence.

In the second case, the client defined the problem and the solution as external to her. The family had tried to have her transfer schools to avoid the feelings of hopelessness prior to moving to their new house. But, the failure of her first transfer developed the girl's inner interpersonal anxiety, and the problem became internal when she entered therapy. In this case, solution-focused therapy in which the girl herself was the agent of the solution was indicated. Treatment of the girl's inner emotional disturbance suggested that the solution was also within herself. To resolve her hopelessness, her positive experience with her puppy was utilized (in the therapy) and externalized as a verbal symbol, which became an effective means of changing the mother–daughter communication. New symbol making was suggested, which externalized her positive part and had her conduct self-directed activity. It seemed that in the process of the symbol making, her anxiety about being isolated in her class was absorbed into the symbol and the symbol gave her confidence.

In both cases, to permit the transformation of the stories through which the clients could shift from being victims to agents, externalized symbols were needed that freed them from their problems and led to solutions. The clients' positive parts were utilized, and their self-directed activity of symbol generation and symbol making provided clues to solve their problems. It seemed that the symbols were built inside them as a part of their new identities.

The Agent's Positive Coping Set

In the first case, the therapist noticed a correlation between the client's imagery and his bodily tension. In the fourth session he moved his left hand to the left side of his neck when he was seeing a weak part of his body image. In the eighth session the therapist intended to change the pattern of the imagery and the client's bodily tension (see Bandler & Grinder, 1979). His left hand on his right shoulder was replaced with the therapist's hand, and the therapist had the boy's right hand move to his left shoulder. Consequently, the client could relax both of his shoulders and he got a clue to change the content of his imagery, at which time he generated a flying saucer. It was clear that the content of his imagery and his actual bodily sensations interacted. When the imaging agent could relax himself even unconsciously, his imagery developed and he saw the flying saucer with a feeling of relief.

From the perspective of imagery analysis, many interpretations are possible. For example, the magicians in the sixth session may be interpreted as the boy's mother and her boyfriend or her ex-husband, or himself and his other self. The box thrown away from the flying saucer may be interpreted as his dependent feeling toward his mother or relief goods from the UFO. In the thirteenth session, the yellow area in the darkness may be a symbol of his integrative self, or literally a star or a UFO. However, it was noted that the relaxed feeling of the imaging agent provided him with a clue to change the imagery. About this issue, Kouno (1992) pointed out that a non-negative experience mode, like comfort and good feeling toward a problem, caused therapeutic effects.

In the second case, the girl's pleasant feeling toward her puppy was utilized and was externalized as a verbal symbol. The task of making an embroidery also was suggested to modify her negative feeling toward school. The girl immediately and eagerly started the embroidery so that she could take it to school with her. Through the activity, the agent could cope with a distressful situation with positive feeling. The agent's positive coping set toward a therapeutic suggestion or task that would lead to the solution changes the agent from passive to active.

As the two cases illustrate, unlike White's approach of "externalizing" (White, 1989), a positive part within the client was utilized—not merely the problem—and externalized as a new symbol through which the clients could cope with their emotional problems. Symbols or symbolic acts can be effective means of treating a client's emotional problem, because they are multidimensional.

References

Bandler, R., & Grinder, J. (1979). *Frogs into princes*. Moab, UT: Real People Press.
de Shazer, S. (1988). *Clues*. New York: Norton.
Erickson, M. H., & Rossi, E. L. (1979). *Hypnotherapy*. New York: Irvington.
Kouno, Y. (1992). Mainly about experience mode. In G. Naruse (Ed.), *Saimin ryohou o kangaeru* [*Thinking of hypnotherapy*]. (pp. 179–198). Tokyo: Seishin.
Sluzki, C. E. (1992). Transformation: A blueprint for narrative changes in therapy. *Family Process, 31*, 217–230.
White, M. (1989). *Selected Papers*. Adelaide, South Australia: Dulwich Centre.
Zeig, J. K. (Ed.). (1980). *A teaching seminar with Milton H. Erickson*. New York: Brunner/Mazel.

The Effects of Therapeutic Stories on Adolescent Behavior Patterns

Harry Vincenzi, Ed.D.

This chapter examines the use of therapeutic stories with students who are underachievers or have behavior problems. The stories were developed using strategies developed by Lankton and Lankton (1986, 1989). The stories were bound in book form and read by students in school classrooms as part of their curriculum. Teachers noticed improved student behavior. There was also a higher percentage of students whose reading grades improved than was found in a control group. There was further evidence of interpersonal behavior changes based on the pretest–posttest results of the Interpersonal Checklist. The 136 students who read the stories self-reported improved interpersonal behavior patterns. The control group self-reported behavior patterns that seemed more problematic than their pretest scores. The trends of the data collected were positive and support the use of therapeutic stories in the classroom. In light of the current inability of school systems to meet the changing needs of students, therapeutic stories can provide needed help to students in the classroom.

This chapter examines the use of Ericksonian approaches to help underachieving students develop the resources they need to succeed within the structure of a middle school classroom.

A story told by John Bradshaw (1990) on public television provides a good introduction to our material. While keeping the context, I have changed and personalized this message from my own experiences. I have been working with the Philadelphia School District for 18 years, and during that time I have been involved with the education of many students. Among them have been a thief, a teenage mother, a prostitute, a drug dealer, and an alcoholic. The thief was a quick-witted boy who sat in the back row and always knew how to get a laugh. The teenage mother was fatherless

Address correspondence to Harry Vincenzi, Ed.D., Future Press, P.O. Box 2569, Bala Cynwyd, PA 19004.

and looked to older men to help her; the prostitute was a rebellious, self-effacing girl who learned to depend more on her alluring smile than on her ability. The drug dealer was a leader, competitive and aggressive, and the alcoholic was a distrustful, angry boy whose behaviors caused him to be placed in special education classes by the third grade.

Today, the thief bounces in and out of prison, and, lacking any skills, he'll be back in jail. The teenage mother lives in a highrise project. She has had five children by four different men, none of whom she sees any more. The prostitute has AIDS, and being beaten has become a common event in her life. The drug dealer was killed in a bar because someone wanted to take over his business, and the alcoholic lives in the streets, panhandling for money.

Unfortunately, their time in school was spent learning how to determine the angles of an octagon and recite passages from *Hamlet*. This story is a sad reminder of what some children are required to learn in school at the expense of what they need to learn.

The point is not to belittle the value of learning any academic subject. However, some students' internal resources must be strengthened before subjects such as geometry can be deemed relevant. Supporting this belief was a recent study (1989) by the Carnegie Council, which indicated that half of all middle school students are at risk for some form of school failure. This means that millions of children are at risk and that the resources currently available are inadequate to deal with the problem. Perhaps there is a common ground, that what children need to learn also can be embedded into the curriculum. That is the crux of this chapter: the possibility that by identifying and understanding the interpersonal patterns adolescents use to create problems, solutions can be modeled for them through short stories. It is time to examine how students create and maintain these problems and to provide some form of intervention. The intervention needs to be accessible to all students and easy to implement in the classroom.

The need for this type of intervention is growing, because there is abundant evidence that efforts to improve schools over the last 25 years have had minimal success (Lytle, 1992). There are many possible reasons for this. Glazer (1992) believes that central bureaucracies should be abolished because they are not innovative or change oriented. Sarason (1990) wrote that educational reform is always couched in terms of improving schools or the quality of education. This implies that educators will do what they have always done, but try to do it better. Lytle (1992) believes that urban school districts are under so much pressure to be considered legitimate institutions that they are ultimately unable to be responsive to their clients (students), because to do so would necessitate radically changing the structure of a school system. Sarason (1990) concluded that if a historical review of the many programs that have come through the educational system and its effects on education were conducted, it would be disheartening. To a large degree, it would be a chronicle of fads. In summary, these educators believe that school systems have been unable to remedy the changing needs of their students. These failings support the necessity for structured changes in the curriculum—ones that will help meet the needs of today's students. The goal would be to build students from within, to help provide them with the resources to succeed within their current environment.

Mental Health and Underachievement

The processes involved in adolescents' learning or behaving at their ability level are complex. Educators usually minimize mental health reasons and assume academic failures are the result of deficiencies in the instructional program (Distad, 1987). This is also the area in which educators have been trained to make changes. Therefore, educators want to solve school problems curricularly. The skills they learned affect their view of the problem. Specifically, educators emphasize the design and implementation of new instructional strategies. They place little weight on the development of mental health strategies that can be incorporated into the classroom. Conversely, psychologists want to solve the problem using their clinical skills. Unfortunately, they develop mental health programs that often do not fit the typical instructional model of a school. This has made the relationship between mental health clinicians and educators difficult, and yet, more than ever, there is a need for them to work together.

There is a growing body of evidence to suggest that how you feel affects how well you can learn. Mental health problems in adolescents have been related to academic underachievement and chronic behavior difficulties (Nieman and Matson, 1989; Vincenzi, 1987). Mufson, Cooper, and Hall (1989) found that underachievers were less self-confident, less socially and emotionally mature, and less hard-working than their achieving peers. When teachers rated the two groups, underachievers also were found to be less goal oriented, had lower self-concepts and were not as responsible. Emlen (1991) believes that constructs such as a fear of success are situation specific—that is, adolescents are going to fail not in general, but in specific areas of their lives. One may feel anxiety not about all competitive activities, only about certain ones.

The results of these and other, earlier studies have led to numerous school-based interventions (e.g., Spivack and Shure, 1974; Comer, 1980). Although they offer excellent tools to deal with problems, these programs have had difficulty being utilized by schools on a large-scale basis: the programs are not easily implemented, require teacher training, and the organizational structure of the school must change. One way to minimize those problems would be to design a cost-efficient mental health intervention, one that teachers would be familiar with and that would not force them into a new role. The use of therapeutic reading stories could be such a tool, because reading is a normal part of the school curriculum.

Method

The goals of this project were:

1. To identify the interpersonal patterns that contribute to adolescent problems such as underachievement and inappropriate behavior
2. To develop a series of therapeutic short stories based on the identified interpersonal patterns that could be integrated into the regular school program
3. To try out the stories in regular classroom situations and assess their effects on student grades and classroom behavior

Teachers and counselors from four middle schools identified 77 students whom they perceived as academic underachievers or chronic behavior problems. The students were assessed in groups of four with the Interpersonal Checklist (ICL; Leary, 1957) and the Emotional/Social Loneliness Inventory (ESLI; Vincenzi and Grabosky, 1987). Each item was read aloud to the students, and definitions were provided for each item. To provide support for the validity of the findings, a one-paragraph description based on the individual student results were made for 30 of the students. The teachers and counselors found that the results from the ICL and the ESLI supported their views concerning those students (Vincenzi, 1991).

Correlations among the ICL subtest findings revealed two statistically significant interpersonal patterns (Vincenzi, 1991). The first pattern indicated that students who tended to be competitive, managerial, and independent were also more likely to be aggressive, hostile, and rebellious. Therefore, when problem students who are competitive and independent encounter a difficult situation, they are more likely to use unfriendly behaviors to try to resolve it. The second pattern indicated that problem students who saw themselves as friendly, cooperative, and supportive were more likely to see themselves as dependent and self-effacing. When those in the second group of students encountered a difficult situation, they may have used submissive behaviors to cope with the problem. Significant differences did not appear between the sexes, indicating that the interpersonal skills used to create or maintain problems were not different for boys and girls.

The student's loneliness scores (ESLI) were used to establish a third pattern. The data indicated that 54% of the students were either emotionally or socially lonely; 22% were both. When the data were analyzed by sex, differences were found. For boys, suspicious and distrustful behaviors were associated with social or emotional loneliness. This agrees with Leary's concept of the interpersonal circle, according to which those behaviors should provoke rejection. For girls, emotional or social loneliness was associated with less confidence and independence. Thus, behaviors that are submissive and docile were more associated with loneliness. The girls were more likely to withdraw from a problem situation, which in turn led to feelings of loneliness.

Based on the above data, a series of short stories was written. The stories were subsequently entitled *Changes* (Vincenzi, 1994).

Metaphor/Short Story Development

The use of storytelling to help others learn is an age-old phenomenon. More recently, Milton Erickson's use of metaphors as a therapeutic intervention has been analyzed and structured (Lankton and Lankton, 1986). The Lanktons have written about the use of metaphors to help change specific behaviors, attitudes, or affects. They have emphasized the use of Leary's Interpersonal Checklist as a diagnostic tool. They use the ICL to identify interpersonal needs in clients. Then, based on the results of the ICL, the interpersonal areas that need to be strengthened or reinforced are embedded in the metaphors. The goal is to create a story with a protagonist who uses the same behavior patterns as the client. The protagonist eventually learns and uses a new set of behaviors to help cope with the problem. Matthews and Langdell (1989) found that clients reported that the use of metaphors helped them to change. Lankton and Lankton (1986) believe that if the metaphors match the client's behavior patterns, the client will unconsciously begin to work on his or her problem with the new resources offered.

The work in the present study emphasized Leary's (1957) model of interpersonal behavior and in particular the interpersonal circle of behaviors. More recently, Lankton and Lankton (1986) and Andrews (1989a, 1989b) have used Leary's model. Andrews's (1989a) work reinforced Leary's concepts of complimentary patterns and self-confirming behaviors. Complimentary patterns deal with compliments and opposites on the interpersonal circle and the behaviors they tend to provoke in others. For example, friendly behaviors provoke friendly behaviors in other people, whereas competitive behaviors will provoke self-effacing behaviors. Andrews (1989b) believes people maintain or create problems through their interpersonal interactions. For example, an adolescent feels rejected because of a series of childhood experiences. He or she may choose to use suspicion and distrust as a protective mechanism. According to Leary (1957) those behaviors will tend to provoke rejection from others and continues the original pattern found in his or her childhood. Andrews (1989b) believes that this behavior pattern is performed unconsciously to help maintain the initial level of self-concept that developed as a result of the first rejection. Lankton and Lankton believe that if a person's self-confirmation strategies can be identified via the ICL, then the appropriate metaphors can be developed. This model implies that problems result from not using or knowing appropriate skills, from the use of behaviors that create a self-fulfilling prophecy, or both.

To help demonstrate the skills students need to learn, short stories in the form of metaphors were developed. The protagonists in the stories may be male or female; both genders are found in more than half the stories. Three types of stories were developed. The first was informational, designed to provide the resources students needed to learn to change their behavior. Two types of resources were offered, the first based on Leary's and Andrews' self-confirmation models. For example, if you are suspicious and distrustful, people will want to reject you. However, if you are supportive and kind, people will want to accept you. These concepts are learned in a story format entitled "The Acting Class–Control." In this story, sets of behaviors must be mastered as a prerequisite to learning to act. People must know how their behaviors affect others and how the others' behaviors affect them. The second type of resource used informs students "how to do" certain behaviors. Using a actual survey of adolescents, students learn specific behaviors that compose a skill such as how to be friendly. Fourteen skills, such as how to be self-confident and how to make a good impression, are offered in two parts in "The Survey Says."

To accomplish the goal of embedding solutions within a series of short stories, a solution-oriented approach was employed along with the use of metaphors. Underlying this concept is the work of de Shazer (1988) and O'Hanlon and Weiner-Davis (1989), which embodies the belief that people do not have problems, they *do* problems. For example, John was labeled an underachiever. If John were, then John would always underachieve, and this is usually not the case. Teachers like to talk of the boys like John who know all the sports statistics but are failing math. So the question is: How does John underachieve? What specific behaviors does John use to underachieve? For example, if in math class John is continually self-effacing (thinking, "I can't do this") and uses no managerial behaviors (e.g., setting time aside to study), then John underachieves. According to the Lanktons' approach, one way to help John is to encourage him to be more competitive and managerial. The first step in doing this is to provide clear, detailed information about how to be more competitive and managerial. This again is the purpose of stories such as "The Survey Says."

The second and third story types contain metaphors and are based on the Lanktons' work (1986). Using the self-confirmation patterns identified by the first study, the stories were designed to help students learn new solutions to their old problems. The second story type dealt with a concept. For example, in the story entitled "Excuses," a young man has an excuse for everything that happens to him. He learns to accept a limitation and in doing so learns to overcome his limitation. He then realizes he no longer needs his excuses. The third type of story involves protagonists who initially use the same behavior patterns as the problem students in the first study. During the course of the story, each protagonist learns a new skill or decides to use different interpersonal behaviors. The result is that the characters change and learn that the new behaviors helped them to resolve their initial problems. All the stories contain an indirect message to change. They may emphasize specific messages (e.g., managerial and angry types need to be more friendly, or friendly but self-effacing types need to do more planning). They utilize the information in the other stories and at times refer to them.

The 15 stories work best when read on a weekly basis. At the end of each story, questions designed to reinforce the messages in the stories are presented. Students were asked to write a paragraph about which skills (from "The Survey Says") would best help the protagonist. Other questions ask students to try a new behavior and note what was different. The most important part was to have students read and comprehend the stories. It was assumed that if the students identified with the protagonists, the stories would be of interest to them. Therefore, an attempt was made to make the stories age appropriate and emphasize themes that would be of interest. Because underachievers can get bored easily, all stories were kept under fifteen pages and written at the fifth-grade level. These steps would ensure a short story that would be easy to read.

Upon completion of the pre-test, the treatment group had complete data for 136 students. These data included the ICL, Student Grades, Student Behavior Grades and Student Effort Ratings. It was decided based on discussions with Steven Lankton (Personal Communication, December 8, 1990) and John Andrews (Personal Communication, December 14, 1990) that related ICL subtests could be subtracted from each other. In this way, for example, if a student was more competitive than self-effacing, a positive score would result. This would help to determine which areas were more dominant and make an analysis of patterns easier. Using Leary's 1975 matrix (see Andrews, 1989a) the following subtests were subtracted form each other. It was assumed that dominant and friendly behaviors would create fewer problems than submissive and unfriendly behaviors.

The second part of the study focused on two schools, a low-income urban school and a middle-class urban school. The 15 stories were bound in book form and given to three teachers at School A and one teacher at School B. School A was a middle-class urban school; School B served a low-income population. In addition, two classes from School A were chosen to serve as a control group. These two classes were matched by grade with two classes in the treatment group from School A. It was not possible to obtain permission to have a control group from School B.

In total, four classes read the stories, while two other classes served as a control group. The ICL was used as a pretest and posttest measure, as were each student's grades.

A–J	Managerial versus Dependent
P–K	Advisor/Teacher versus Seeks Help/Depends On
B–I	Confident/Independent versus Weak/Submissive
C–H	Competitive versus Self-Effacing
O–D	Responsible/Helpful versus Sarcastic/Unkind
N–E	Supportive versus Unfriendly
M–F	Affectionate versus Rebellious/Complaining
L–G	Cooperative versus Suspicious/Distrustful

Results

When student grades and effort ratings were analyzed, the results revealed a positive correlation of .91. This very high correlation indicates that if students were perceived by the teacher as trying, it is unlikely that these students would receive a low grade. It further implies that generally, teachers believe that most low-achieving students are underachievers.

Students (by their grades and behavior ratings) were divided into four categories and analyzed by their ICL ratings (Table 1). The categories were students who had good grades and good behavior ratings, students with average grades and good behavior ratings, students who had low grades and good behavior ratings, and students who had low grades and bad behavior ratings. The results indicated the following:

Table 1
Breakdown of the Treatment Group by Academic Grades, Behavior Ratings, and ICL Scores

A–J	B–I	P–K	C–H	O–D	N–E	L–G	M–F	Acad. Grd	Behavior Rating	N
.61	5.2	4.9	2.30	3.20	2.1	-.60	2.3	B	Good	23
-1.10	2.1	3.8	.43	.84	1.0	.61	.2	C	Good	49
-3.60	1.2	2.7	-2.00	1.00	3.0	.88	-.5	D	Good	17
.13	3.3	4.5	-.20	-.50	-.7	-.30	-1.9	D	Poor	47

1. Students with good grades and good behavior ratings were independent, responsible, and competitive, and a little rebellious; however, they were also found to be friendly and cooperative (i.e., had positive values on A–J, O–D, C–H, and L–G).
2. Students with average grades and good behavior ratings were more dependent than independent but well balanced in all the other categories (had a negative value on A–J).
3. Students with low grades and good behavior ratings were found to be very dependent and self-effacing (had negative values on A–J and C–H).
4. Students with low grades and bad behavior ratings were found to be independent and managerial but also self-effacing, sarcastic, hostile, and distrustful (i.e., had positive values on A–J and B–I, but negative values on C–H, O–D, M–F, and L–G).

These findings indicated that students who were labeled underachievers or behavior problems used interpersonal patterns that were different from and less effective than those of their higher-achieving peers. This type of analysis revolves around which interpersonal skills are self-reported as more dominant. That means that although high-achieving students can also be self-effacing or distrustful, their dominant traits are to be competitive and cooperative. Conversely, low-achieving students can be cooperative, but their dominant traits are such behaviors as being distrustful. This in turn is likely to create rejection from others (teachers and peers) and continue the cycle. These data corroborated the information provided by the first study. They support the belief that the interpersonal patterns used by students are related to problems in their lives, such as underachievement.

Because of organizational problems, the schools did not start using the stories until November 1991. They completed the stories in early June 1992. This schedule did not keep to the original plan of completing the stories in

19 weeks, beginning in October. However, the schedule may reflect the reality of using a supplemental reader in a school system. The degree to which each teacher used the stories also differed. Some stories were simply read by the students, others were used for discussion, and some were used to examine the main idea in the story. In general, teachers did not take the time to have students individually answer in writing the end-of-story questions. This lack of reinforcement by teachers may be considered a limitation, but it may also reflect the realities that occur in the classroom. This was a deliberate part of the study, in that teachers were given clear guidelines and instructions but were also allowed to use the stories as they would use materials under normal conditions. Although this procedure has its drawbacks, it eliminates the problem of having something succeed under artificial conditions. All too often in education, a study will produce excellent results, but then cannot be replicated when the concept is "packaged" and sent to other schools.

During the school year, the researcher meet with the teachers to obtain feedback about the use of the stories in the classroom. In general, the feedback was extremely positive. The teachers indicated that they liked the stories and saw the need for stories of this nature. They also indicated that the students looked forward to and enjoyed reading the stories.

Toward the end of the school year, a reporter for the *Philadelphia Inquirer* interviewed one teacher and her students (Mezzacapa, 1992). Some of the responses from the students were: "They give you ideas and things to change to. If your attitude is bad, the idea is to change and better yourself." "The stories tell us about us." "You get to understand who you are." The teacher felt that she "didn't get as many sleepers and everybody wants to be involved."

At the end of the school year, each of the teachers wrote a letter about his or her experience using the stories. One stated, "I have used this program with my sixth-grade students and have seen them as well as heard them take the initiative to avoid as well as settle disputes among themselves and others." Another stated that "this program opened opportunities for discussion of specific problems both individually and in small groups." A third teacher added, "I noticed a change in attitude as a result of what they had read and reacted to in the stories."

These comments reflect the feelings of teachers and students who have had an opportunity to experience reading *Changes*. This does not mean every student loved the stories or benefitted from them. It does mean that the stories were well received and that stories of this nature can influence student behavior.

The data were analyzed to locate trends in the effects of the stories. Statistical procedures were not used, for two reasons:

1. The subtraction of the ICL subtest scores from one another raises questions as to what constitutes a real difference.
2. The use of eight subtest scores requires that patterns, rather than individual differences be examined on each subtest.

The treatment and control group comparisons involved only the seventh and eighth grade students in School A. Of the students in the treatment group, 43% improved their reading grades between the first and last marking periods. In comparison, only 27% of the students in the control group improved their grades. For the treatment group, 6% showed a decline in grades, compared to 8% for the control group.

There were no real differences in behavior grades between the treatment and control groups. This finding did not support the comments made by the teachers, who in general saw an improvement in behavior. The results from the ICL were more supportive of the teachers' comments.

The pretest results (Table 2) indicated that the control group (based on average ICL scores) had a better profile than the treatment group. Thus, whereas both groups seemed more dependent than independent, the treatment group was more self-effacing and less trusting. However, when the posttest results were examined, it was found that the treatment group had a much healthier profile. The treatment group (again, based on average ICL scores) had become more independent and less self-effacing, but this was also true of the control group. The difference was that the treatment group saw themselves as more cooperative, trusting, and friendly. This was the type of balance that the metaphors were designed to model for students. Equally important was the fact that the control group's posttest profile contained the potential for more behavior problems: although they became more independent, competitive, and managerial, they also became more aggressive, unfriendly, rebellious, and distrustful. In light of these findings, the treatment group's teachers comments about better behavior on the part of their students are easier to understand.

Table 2
Pretest and Posttest ICL Results for the Treatment and Control Group

	A–J	B–I	P–K	C–H	O–D	N–E	L–G	M–F
				Treatment Group				
Pre	-1.0	3.4	4.0	-.02	1.0	.8	1.6	-.30
Post.	1.6	2.3	1.5	1.20	-.8	-.2	1.4	.99
				Control Group				
Pre	-1.70	2.6	3.8	.2	.98	.44	1.4	1.6
Post.	.42	4.1	4.2	2.0	-.70	-1.90	-.6	-.8

Summary

The above results reflect group trends rather than an analysis of individual students. However, the findings imply that student behavior can be altered by modeling solutions for them via their reading materials. It is possible to offer mental health strategies and embed them within the normal school curriculum. This approach has the advantages of reaching a broad-based audience and not disrupting the normal school day. It does not require teachers to act like clinicians and allows them to focus their energy on instructional change. This type of change should also appeal to school systems, which have had limited success in implementing instructional programs that successfully alter student achievement and behavior. Perhaps in conjunction with a curriculum that helps to build the child from within, instructional programs have a better chance of succeeding.

Note that the goal was not to prove that one set of stories would complete the task of changing the students' behaviors. However, the fact that teachers and students reported differences supports the contention that changes can occur using this format. If stories of this nature were made part of the curriculum, students could have numerous strategies modeled and reinforced for them over the secondary school years. Such an approach would allow us to reach out to those students who normally would not receive any help from the mental health community. The improved student behavior and academic performance that can be a result of this strategy should appeal most to educators. This is of growing importance as educators are being stymied by instructional strategies that have had little impact and myriad social problems that are beyond their control.

The last 25 years have shown the difficulty of developing effective instructional strategies; however, stories in *Changes* offer an innovative way to reach out to students. If an entire curriculum were developed, students could learn at an early age how to alter the behavior patterns they use that create and maintain problems in their lives. Then perhaps the lives of the potential thief, teenage mother, prostitute, drug dealer, and alcoholic could be changed.

References

Andrews, J. (1989a, May). Integrating visions of reality, interpersonal diagnosis and existential vision. *American Psychologist, 44*, 803–817.

Andrews, J. (1989b). The psychotherapy of depression: A self-confirmation model. *Psychological Review, 96*, 576–607.

Bradshaw, J. (Speaker). (1990). *The eight seasons of man* [Videotaped series]. Public Broadcasting System, WHYY, Philadelphia, PA.

Carnegie Council on Adolescent Development. (1989, June). *Turning points: Preparing American youth for the 21st century.* Carnegie Corporation of New York.

Comer, J. (1980). *School power.* New York: Free Press.

de Shazer, S. (1988). *Clues: Investigating solutions in brief therapy.* New York: Norton.

Distad, L. (1987, June). A personal legacy. *Phi Delta Kappan,* 744–746.

Emlen, J. (February, 1991). Achievement orientation in early adolescence: Developmental patterns and social correlates. *Journal of Early Adolescence, 11,* 125–151.

Glazer, N. (1992, October 4). , The consuming passion of Constance Clayton. *Philadelphia Inquirer, Inquirer Magazine ,* 20–30. Philadelphia, PA.

Lankton, C., & Lankton, S. (1989). *Tales of enchantment: Goal-oriented metaphors for adults and children in therapy.* New York: Brunner/Mazel.

Lankton, S., & Lankton, C. (1986). *Enchantment and intervention in family therapy.* New York: Brunner/Mazel.

Leary, T. (1957). *The interpersonal diagnosis of personality.* New York: Norton.

Lytle, J. (1992, July). Prospects for reforming urban schools. *Urban Education, 27,* 109–131.

Matthews, W., & Langdell, S. (1989, April). What do clients think about the metaphors they receive: An initial inquiry. *American Journal of Clinical Hypnosis, 27,* 242–251.

Mezzacapa, D. (1992, March 19). Helping kids relate to reading. *Philadelphia Inquirer,* B1.

Mufson, L., Cooper, J., & Hall, J. (1989, September). Factors associated with underachievement in seventh grade children. *Journal of Educational Research,* 5–10.

Nieman, G., & Matson, J. (1989, Summer). Depressive problems in conduct disordered adolescents. *Journal of School Psychology, 27,* 175–188.

O'Hanlon, W., & Weiner-Davis, M. (1989). *In search of solutions.* New York: Norton.

Sarason, S. (1990). *The predictable failure of educational reform.* San Francisco: Jossey-Bass.

Spivack, G., & Shure, M. (1974). *Social adjustment of young children: A cognitive approach to solving real-life problems.* San Francisco: Jossey-Bass.

Vincenzi, H. (1987, Summer). Relationship between depression and reading ability in sixth grade children. *Journal of School Psychology, 25,* 155–160.

Vincenzi, H. (1991, June). *Adolescent interpersonal patterns and adolescent problems: Developing a school based intervention.* Paper presented at the National Conference on the Teaching of Social Competency Skills, New London, CT.

Vincenzi, H., & Grabosky, F. (1987). Measuring the emotional/social aspects of loneliness and isolation. *Journal of Social Behavior and Personality, 2,* 257–270.

Vincenzi, H. (1994). *Changes.* Bala Cynwyd, PA: Future Press.

How Ambiguous Are Ambiguous Tasks?

Marc Franchot Weiss, Ph.D.

It has been conjectured that some of Dr. Erickson's tasks were vague, ambiguous, metaphoric, symbolic and/or served a projective function. Anecdotal research on a standardized ambiguous function assignment (task) (Lankton & Lankton, 1986) given to over 30 patients is presented. In most cases the behavioral and cognitive responses were quite different, but at times there were some common responses. It is conjectured that some of Dr. Erickson's "ambiguous" tasks had a not so ambiguous intent. A structure is provided to differentiate between "ambiguous" tasks and "diagnostic" tasks.

What do mountains, hammers, jars, treats, restaurants, and clips all have in common? Yes, they all end with the letter s. Yes, they all are plurals. No, they are not all things you can put in your pocket! Yes, that is right! You have it now! They all "objects" that can be used in the creation of therapeutic tasks. Before we examine these "objects" and their related tasks, let us review the precedents of task usage.

Magical Acts and Rituals

Since the days of ancient doctors, healers, wizards, and magicians, assignments, tasks, rituals, and acts have been employed for the creation of many and yet very specific results, including the creation of allusions, the creation of illusions, the suspension of beliefs, and the development of climactic, magnificent effects. There seem to be three core elements related to the tasks, acts, and rituals: (a) *spells*, or incantations, which are spoken formulas; (b) *rites*, which are sets of formalized actions; and (c)

Address correspondence to Marc Weiss, Ph.D., Milton H. Erickson, Institute of Northern Illinois, 2421 W. Pratt Blvd., Suite 214, Chicago, IL 60659.

certain *objects* believed to be endowed with magical power. Mixed together, these ingredients become the potion that stimulates, excites, and leaves people amazed. Together, these elements create the ceremony in all its splendor, wondrousness, majesty, and aura.

The *spell* is the most important part of the ceremony and may sometimes be used alone. It may be a long and intricate passage, a few phrases, or even a single word or group of syllables, sometimes meaningless, like "abracadabra," which magicians borrowed from Arabian tales. The spell may be in an ordinary or a secret language. A spell usually calls on powerful gods and mythical ancestors for support.

The *rite*, almost always accompanied by a spell, may involve dance or pantomimes that act out the desired result. For example, to bring good luck in hunting, the Indians of ancient Mexico performed a dance imitating a deer shot by arrows. Rites may also be actions without apparent meaning that are believed to cause or prevent certain events or heighten the effect of the ceremony.

The *objects* used may be natural, such as stones, water, or a tree branch. Their powers are often believed to be inherent. Some natural objects and all artificial objects (such as spears, drums, and carved figures), are enchanted or given magical power by having a spell said over them. Objects, such as water or a spear, are major items in ceremonies. Others, called amulets, charms, or fetishes, may be worn or carried for protection against bad luck, disasters, or other evils. In the Middle Ages, for instance, it was believed that amber worn over the heart prevented epilepsy and that an amethyst warded off drunkenness.

Homeopathic magic (Burlingame, 1974; Nelms, 1969) is based on the belief that like produces like. In this type of magic, also called imitative magic, magicians act out or imitate what they want to happen. They often use a model or miniature of whatever they want to influence. For example, a fisherman may make a model of a fish and pretend he is netting it. It is believed this ritual will assure a good catch. In some European folk dances, the dancers leap high into the air to make their crops grow tall. People once believed that a yellow flower would cure jaundice, a yellowish discoloration of the body.

Many taboos come from homeopathic magic. People avoid certain harmless things because they resemble various harmful things. For example, Eskimo parents might warn their sons against playing a string game, such as cat's cradle, in which children loop string around their fingers. It was believed playing such games might cause the children's fingers to become tangled in the harpoon lines they will use as adults.

Contagious magic (Burlingame, 1974; Nelms, 1969) comes from the belief that after a person has had contact with certain things, those things will continue to influence that person. The most common examples of contagious magic involve parts of the body that have been removed, such as fingernails, hair, and teeth. A person's nails and hair supposedly can affect the rest of that person's body long after they have been cut off. A person can injure an enemy by damaging a lock of hair or a piece of clothing. An enemy can be crippled by placing a sharp object in that person's footprint. People who believe in contagious magic fear that an enemy can gain power over them by obtaining parts of their body; therefore, they carefully dispose of their nails, hair, teeth, and even their body wastes.

Parallels can be made to psychotherapy, which often involves some form of spells and actions. Some therapies even use objects. Think about systematic and live/in vivo desensitization process, guided imagery, role playing, and so forth. Do we not assume that the rehearsal of actions, either in the imagination or in reality, dissipates anxiety and changes attitudes and beliefs? Do we not try to model what we want our patients to be like? Similarly, do we not warn our patients about a variety of things because of the ill effects of such actions or thoughts?

If nothing else, rituals and ceremonies have been used by societies and cultures to mark the passage of one developmental stage to another. Let us now consider those acts, rituals, and tasks so commonly employed by systems, family, strategic, solution, and Ericksonian therapists. Perhaps, as Haley (1984) has implied, therapy in and of itself is a task and therefore curative.

There is extensive coverage elsewhere of the nature, use, and construction of paradoxical tasks, skill-building tasks, ambiguous tasks, and a variety of therapeutic rituals. For more detailed information, the reader is urged to review, for example, de Shazer (1985), Fisch, Weakland, and Segal (1982), Frankl (1939, 1975), Haley (1973a, 1973b), Lankton and Lankton (1983, 1986), Madaness (1981, 1984), O'Hanlon (1987), Palazzoli, Boscolo, Cecchin, and Prata (1978), van der Hart (1981), Weeks (1982), and Weiss (1992). The intent here is to examine those therapeutic tasks that have been considered "ambiguous" and therefore "projective."

A Return to Our Question

What do clips, hammers, treats, mountains, restaurants, and jars all have in common? Let us examine each.

Mountains

One of Erickson's favorite tasks or at least frequently mentioned was to "go climb Squaw Peak." You might ask what that would have to do with anything. Perhaps this was, as frequently believed, a rather vague or ambiguous task that would result in individualized meaning for anyone who performed it. Perhaps Erickson had a much more specific intent than we will ever know.

Let us examine one often-mentioned case (Gordon & Meyers-Anderson, 1981; O'Hanlon and Hexum, 1990; Zeig, 1980). A psychiatrist who had been practicing for 30 years without building a successful practice and his wife went to Dr. Erickson for marital therapy. Each had been in analysis for a number of years. On the first day, Dr. Erickson sent the husband to climb Squaw Peak and the wife to visit the Botanical Gardens. They returned. The husband had a wonderful report, and the wife had hated her excursion. On the second day, the wife was sent to Squaw Peak and the husband to the Botanical Gardens. Again, the husband was thrilled and the wife had nothing positive to report. On the third day, they independently chose their own destinations, Squaw Peak or the Botanical Gardens. The husband returned to the Botanical Gardens and the wife to Squaw Peak. They returned to Dr. Erickson, who stated that their therapy was over.

After returning home to Pennsylvania, they both terminated psychoanalysis and went out independently. The wife filed for divorce. The husband worked on his practice. Both were reported to be happier. Obviously this account does not include the context within which Dr. Erickson prescribed the assignment, nor does it have his spell, patter, or exact words, which may have influenced or focused the couple's experience. Even one sentence reported by Gordon and Meyers-Anderson (1981, p. 94), "Being that the landscape is a lot different than Philadelphia then you ought to *discover* a few things about the world in which you *live*," may have altered the experience. We can take the position that either Dr. Erickson created an ambiguous task for the purpose of discovery, insight, and involvement, or the task had a specific purpose of pointing out "irreconcilable differences" between the couple, or both. Yes, perhaps the task was both ambiguous and had a specific intent.

O'Hanlon and Hexum (1990) believe the task was behavioral (to be done between sessions) and symbolic (problem symbolization). Based upon their definition, it seems that the exercise was, at least from my point of view, ambiguous and projective. However, I have some anecdotal evidence, a bit ludicrous, that may lend some credence that this was Erickson's "divorce/be happier alone" task. Let us examine this ludicrous proof, so we consider all options before making a conclusion.

Mountains Revisited

In 1981 I treated a man for many sessions for chronic depression. It seemed Len's depression was related to his separation from his wife, Helen.

Helen refused to come to any of our sessions. There were repeated over-
tures by both Len and myself. She never would come; perhaps her position told the whole story.

At one session, Len seemed almost in a manic condition. He was elated.
He was joyous. He was overwhelmed with the effect of therapy. Helen
suddenly agreed to come to one session and consider a reconciliation. I
have no recollection of how or why this happened. Subsequently, they sat
in my office beaming at each other much like newlyweds. They announced
they were going on a second honeymoon and would be visiting Len's father in Phoenix. The wheels started grinding. I looked at them and said, "I
have something I want you to do when you get to Phoenix. Call me when
you are there." They called and I issued the directive: "Len, climb Squaw
Peak. Being that the landscape is a lot different than Chicago then you
ought to *discover* a few things about the world in which you *live*. Helen, go
to the Botanical Gardens....Call in the morning." Len had positive reports
about Squaw Peak; Helen hated the Gardens. The next directive was—
well, you guessed it. They called the next morning. Len loved the Botanical Gardens; Helen hated Squaw Peak. The next directive was, of
course....They called the next morning. Len loved the Botanical Gardens; Helen still hated Squaw Peak! Wow, is this what is supposed to
happen? I told them their therapy was over, and to call me in a month.
She filed for divorce; he accepted it. His depression seemed to lift; he
started dating and got a job promotion. He still had some contact with
Helen, and she was reported to be happier. Was this Dr. Erickson's divorce: make-them-happier, advance-the-husband's-career task? Or was
it perhaps more accurately "common" problems that resulted in "common" projections and "common" actions in similar contexts? It happened twice! Ludicrous or not, there is no real way of knowing. Perhaps
we need to realize that ambiguous assignments and tasks (a) may have a
diagnostic value to determine motivation for treatment; (b) may, as do
many commonly used projective techniques, have common "pull" in
terms of content and experiences and diagnostic categories; (c) may be
focused, directed, influenced, and limited by the context, manner of
presentation, and context of therapy; or (d) are really diagnostic, skill-
building, or paradoxical tasks for example that are somewhat vague—
or all of these. Given any context, people do impose their "selves" upon
and in it. The patient is the one who makes it metaphoric or symbolic.
After all, just because the therapist thinks it is that way does not make it
so. The patient makes it so. That takes care of one item on our list, mountains. We need to consider the global category of projection and projective
techniques before continuing.

Projective Techniques

The theory of projection is something quite different from the psychoanalytic concept of projection, in which a person attributes or ascribes to the environment, another person, or an object what resides in one's self in order to defend the ego. For our purposes, *projection* is a perceptual process in which a person experiences a figure, image, idea, or object as an objective reality, and it is the psychological process in which the self is reflected.

One of the most common projective techniques used by psychologists is the Thematic Apperception Test (TAT), in which an examinee is shown a series of ambiguous pictures, many of which include human figures. There are 32 possible stimulus cards, and most frequently the examiner chooses 10, based on personal preference, the "pull" or theme that the card allegedly represents, or both. Parenthetically, this may mean that the cards are really not so ambiguous after all or that there is some consensus as to at least a variety of contents that these representations and or renderings may stimulate. The examinee is asked to create a story with three components—the past, the present, and the future—about the picture. There are qualitative and quantitative scoring systems, folklore, and so forth about the meanings and interpretations of themes, interactions and specific content of these stories. From this information a person's needs, press (environmental factors), motivations, and dynamics are deciphered. Another popular test, the Rorschach (Ink Blot), uses 10 cards, some of which are multicolored. The examinee is asked to tell what he or she sees.

Ambiguous function assignments (AFA)(Lankton and Lankton, 1984, 1986) are seemingly based on this same theory of projection used in projective testing techniques employed by psychologists. However, an AFA seems more like the TAT. An ambiguous function assignment seems to create a real-life TAT into and upon which patients project their concerns, beliefs, conflicts, and insights. With and through the skilful questioning of the therapist, the person gains "insight" and "understanding." Being interactive and free flowing rather than descriptive, an AFA would therefore be therapeutic in addition to diagnostic. If nothing else, an AFA in most cases seems to stimulate patients' thoughts and actively engages them in the therapeutic process. An AFA may also make things that are "known" concrete and tangible rather than abstract and obtuse. An AFA permits a wide variety of multidimensional responses. It provides a rich information with a minimum of awareness of the purpose on the patient's part. As Socrates said, "Knowledge is not learned until it is experienced." Perhaps an AFA does just that! Let us return to our list.

Hammers

Several years ago I treated a man who had a long history of agorapho-
bia and a variety of treatment failures. He was told to walk around his
dining room table for two minutes a day. He was told to walk one minute
clockwise and one minute counterclockwise. Over a period of weeks, the
time was significantly increased. He was later told to wear a coat and
hat when performing his assignment. The purpose of walking around
the table was alluded to, and it was stated that there was also something special, something therapeutic, to be learned by also carrying the
heaviest hammer he could find and swinging it as he walked around
the table.

The first intent was to deal with some of the agoraphobic symptoms.
After working with many agoraphobics over the years, I believed that
some of their physiological complaints that are usually taken to be in-
dications of anxiety are really the effect of a lack of exercise.
Agoraphobics usually sit, watch television, chat on the phone, and so
forth. They do very little walking and are not accustomed to the feeling
of fatigue. They are not accustomed to wearing outdoor clothing. The
intent here was obvious: to build strength, stamina, endurance, adaptation, and preparation for the outdoors. Forget the anxiety and panic—
how could someone walk and stand outside for any length of time if
unable to do it inside? Thus, this task, in part, entailed skill building,
preparation, and adaptation and was quite literal and behavioral in
nature.

However, there was a second part to this assignment. The hammer com-
ponent was intended to be ambiguous. The patient called saying he did
not think any of the hammers he had at home was heavy enough. He
started making calls and getting information about hammers. It seems
the standard hammer is 14 ounces, the professional hammer is 16
ounces, and an industrial hammer is 18 ounces. The patient said he had
gotten so angry that "I almost went out of the house to get the one
heavy hammer I could find." That alone would have been interesting!
During one phone call, a salesman asked why such a heavy hammer
was needed. The patient responded, "Because my psychiatrist told me
to get one." The salesman hung up. When I debriefed the patient, he
theorized about the hammer, "It is all this weight I have been carrying
around for years, I have to get rid of it." (The man was obese, and shortly
thereafter put himself on a diet and had realizations that his agorapho-
bia was self-image related. Now, I assume the same realization could
have come from carrying a crow-bar, a heavy book, or for that matter a
paper clip.) The clip will be dealt with later. We have considered mountains and hammers; now the *jars*.

Some Anecdotal Research

The three-jar task originated when I was working with a 26-year-old man who was experiencing panic attacks. He sought me out specifically for hypnotherapy. He was a bit surprised when I had a task for him to perform between sessions. I issued a paradoxical directive to bring on panic attacks after he got to work. His panic attacks usually occurred when he was leaving home or leaving work. He liked the idea of an assignment so much, he asked for something additional to do. I thought I would take a chance. Sometimes, you can lose too much therapeutic leverage by giving too "big" an assignment, or too many assignments at the same time, but he seemed motivated. I thought for a moment. I noticed three jars on a shelf in the office, and I created the "jar assignment."

The assignment was to find three bottles, jars, or containers that were clear and had lids. Then, the jars were to be filled halfway with water. The water in two of the three jars was to be colored different colors. An option was to color all three, so long as they were all different colors. The colors were to be of the patient's choice. The three jars were then to be placed one behind another in a secret place. They were to be stared at five minutes a day, in either the morning, afternoon, or evening. Each day the position of the bottles was to be rotated. On the third day he was to take the bottles and hold them next to each other in his hands (it had been explained earlier that the bottles would have to be small enough for that to be possible) and held up toward the light (preferably natural, but artificial would suffice). The bottles were to be put back in the secret place, and the 3-day cycle and rotation to be continued on, until he was told to stop. It was stated that he would learn something about himself and his situation from this activity.

When he returned for a second hypnotherapy session, he presented himself as a very different person. He seemed confident, he walked tall and straight; he spoke in an assertive manner. He said, "We don't need to do the hypnosis today. I'm cured and I only came because I have a present for you." I asked what made the difference. He said, "You knew all along the jars would do it." I responded, "Well, of course...and what did you learn?" He responded, "I don't need the attacks...anymore. There was the day I forgot to rotate the jars...and I realized things can be the same way on all days." I asked, "What do you mean?" He said, "You know...the jars help me create trance by myself and I can do it [at] any time now...I can handle it as I want...I left the jars as they were on a very good day...and forgot to change it. I realized I was like the water, locked up [at work] too much!" I heard from the man several months later; he said he was doing very well and became a traveling salesman.

I began to use this assignment routinely, and kept track of the variety of responses obtained. To date it has been used more than 30 times, most frequently with striking results. Try it and see what you get! The following select case summaries and responses, presented in edited fashion, provide an overview of those results.

Getting a Handle on a Compromising Situation

A 38-year-old female sought therapeutic assistance to deal with business and relationship matters. The woman had in a short period become a successful entrepreneur in the real estate business. She had opened her own firm and hired many former colleagues and friends to be a part of her rapidly growing organization. The most pressing problem was how to handle an affair with an employee without destroying her marriage of four years. Anxiety and masked depressive symptoms were prominent, as well as degenerating health marked by cardiovascular problems. The patient related many of the problems to the affair but did not know how to get out of it.

A joint session with the "gentleman" was suggested. After the session the patient retracted everything that was said to the gentleman about the nature of the affair. The affair continued. The cardiac symptoms continued to worsen. Medical evaluation indicated no problems other than perhaps a stress or psychosomatic response.

We began some hypnotic work, which was helpful, but the breakthrough followed the three-jar task. The patient revealed the jars helped create a trance-like state while she stared at them and she stated, "It's hard to handle more than one jar at a time and I realized it is hard to handle more than one man at a time." Again, the jars helped create trance, but the "insight" was different.

Three Women: Which to Choose

An attorney sought my assistance for dealing with impotence of six months' duration. He was divorced but dating his former wife. He was also dating one of the secretaries at the law firm where he was employed. Additionally, he was dating one of his clients. He was aware of the ethical and conduct problems in which he was involved, but according to him "the pressing problem is impotence!"

Hypnotic work was the focus of our four sessions. Metaphorically, the ethical situation was also dealt with during these sessions during ostensible treatment of the sexual dysfunction alone. The breakthrough came with the jar task. When the task was completed the young attorney had an interesting story. I first asked about the colors he had used. He had colored the water yellow, red, and brown. I asked about the meaning or significance of those colors. He responded, "None." I instructed him to think more about it. He went on to describe how while he was holding the three jars to the light, one had fallen and broken. He added, "And that is when I saw the light...yes...that's what the colors are about: The brown is for my [ex-]wife, she is a brunette; the yellow is the blonde secretary; and the red is...my client is an Indian [Native American]! I dropped the red one— boy, am I stupid. I shouldn't have gotten involved with her, but I now realize that I can't handle all three!" My response was, "Yes, that's good but perhaps there is just a bit more there!" He said, "You know I brought the bottles with me; let me look again." He had two bottles and quickly surmised, "The brown faded, just like our love. It's over!" This is another interesting response to the jars.

Forgive and Forget

A 46-year-old divorced woman contacted me after many years of therapy. The previous therapy dealt with the period when she, as a child, was sexually and emotionally abused by her father. The childhood memories seemed to have been exacerbated by a recent visit to the family home. Her father was terminally ill and had apparently asked to see his daughter. She visited, and upon her return to the local area, she began having nightmares, panic attacks, and flashbacks. She sought treatment. There was also another problem: she had been called by the family, who had said, "He only has a few more days. He wants to see you, because he says he needs to apologize." We did a hypnotherapy session in which "jars" were casually mentioned (see the Integrative Model, Weiss, 1992). She was given the jar assignment and told to call either as needed or upon her return home. She reported, "I could only see the jar in front of me and yet could see through all three jars in the top half. It seems things are what they are...the color doesn't change...just my associations of what I make of them." After many interesting comments she concluded, "Initially in hypnosis I would have blank spots....I see things differently now...and don't even have the words for it. I'm in touch differently....The exercise was to drive a point home I already know....Life as you see it!" She had further realizations about herself, her former marriage, her newfound ability to sleep, but in the end stated, "Every person is 90 percent water, more than was in the jars; let him rest in peace and so will I."

The Not So Rural Cowboy

A 23-year-old man requested hypnotherapy to help him enhance his ability as a salesman and consultant. He was a self-employed computer software developer, computer programmer, and consultant in a one-man organization. He realized he had become too involved in development and not enough in public relations and promotional work. He wanted help, and hypnotherapy especially, to increase his contractual work, total revenues, and software sales. He also wanted to increase the number of productive hours he worked each week. He spoke of difficulties attending parties, social events, presentation meetings, and the like. He spoke of some insecurities and being a "junior languishing in the shadow of my father." With all this, he revealed his net income for the prior year was 60 thousand dollars. His goal was to triple his net income the next year and to double it for each of the subsequent five years and then retire. Although this was his "fantasy," in reality he was a high school dropout and perhaps had realized much more fantasy than many others.

We did some hypnotherapy work over six sessions, and several tasks were administered. The only one that was promptly completed was—you guessed it—the three jars. Although he was quite bright, he was not very verbal, but he did conclude the following: "I realized that I was devoting too much energy to business and not enough to myself. When I have some fun, I do better in business." Although it took a full hour to extract this interpretation from him, the impetus was his description of the three jars. They were of three different sizes and filled to different levels. One symbolically became work (the largest jar, filled almost to the top), another became family (an intermediate-sized jar that was almost empty) and the other became play. Play was the smallest jar and had just a few drops of water in it, but more than the intermediate jar. He was subsequently given another ambiguous function assignment that included riding a horse. This seemed reasonable because he did wear cowboy boots. Of his own accord, he took the jars with him, and when he returned he symbolically displayed the three jars, all containing identical amounts of water. He concluded, "Even though one thing [work] can be the biggest part of your life, it shouldn't be any more important than anything else." He terminated treatment shortly thereafter and said he was going into partnership with his father.

How Many Sides Does a Cube Have? Let's Count One More Time

A 40-year-old man was referred by his wife, a local health professional with whom I had some professional contact. He had several years of a variety of therapies, including meditation, Zen Buddhism, psychoanalysis, and massage therapy. He sought treatment to work on "several issues which interfaced with writing a self-help book on anxiety and getting things done easily." The patient had seven master's degrees in a variety of subjects, including computer science, business, mathematics, and anthropology. He worked as an accounting clerk following the dissolution of his father's small manufacturing and distribution business. His multifaceted interests included hypnosis, intellectual conversation, and contemplation.

He was given the three-jar assignment. He wrote a prolific manuscript regarding his experiences with what he called the "cubes." In essence, it was a diary of his experiences. He took 7 weeks to find the perfect "cubes," using materials from a chemistry laboratory to measure an identical amount of liquid into each of the cubes, etc. There was also the consideration of what type of water should be used: tap, distilled, carbonated. He spoke of all the pros and cons of each. There were questions regarding coloring, matching, hues, highlights, transparency, and so forth. There were issues regarding the comparison of the cubes on many successive days, because, after all, even controlled indoor lighting varies from day to day. Obviously, the patient's debriefing was quite laborious and drawn out, but it was highlighted by "I make a project out of a project. I procrastinate too much. I wonder what I might miss in life?" To an outsider, this all seemed quite obvious, but to him it must not have. This "insight" became quite concrete to someone who was quite, if not too, abstract. He created his own paradox with the task. For follow-up I see him about once every 18 to 24 months when he is in "crisis." Quite unexpectedly, his wife died about two years later. He recovered more quickly than anyone else I have ever witnessed. He pulled his life together rapidly, got a new job, and even realized he could do that without completing another degree. He enrolled in another master's degree program and was making more rapid progress as a part-time student than he previously had, several times over, as a full-time student. When he received a better starting job offer than others with experience and a relevant degree, he attributed it to the "cubes" and what he learned from them. About five years have passed, and he still refers to the "cubes for support and guidance."

Serial and Simultaneous Ambiguous Function Assignments

In using ambiguous function assignments, I realized that one need not limit oneself to just one such assignment. In fact, if several were given, much like TAT cards, there would be either some new material developed or some validation of what already had been learned. Additional tasks also would be helpful if an initial task was done incorrectly or not done at all. An alternative to serial presentation would be simultaneous presentation of tasks. This is a clinical decision, but it must be realized that one chance with one task may not be enough. Just because it is ambiguous does not mean that it will be projected upon.

Diagnostic and Motivational Assignments

One of the effects that I have discovered in using ambiguous function assignments relates to people who do not do the assignment. They usually have no intention of doing the task, and for that matter have no intention of changing. When you ask them, they usually and ultimately state they do not wish to change; they just wish to know "why I do what I do." I realized that a task could be diagnostic rather than therapeutic. I also realized that Erickson would give a task to assess motivation. Maybe that is what the psychiatrist and his wife and mountains and botanical gardens were really all about.

Treats

Dr. Erickson saw a young couple with marital problems (O'Hanlon and Hexum, 1990). He told them to share a quart of ice cream while sitting on their front steps. Then, they were to return. They had not done the task; Erickson told them their therapy was over and to write to him in one year. A year later he was informed they were divorced. Erickson's rationale was that if the couple did not have enough energy to eat ice cream, they did not have enough energy to solve their marital problems.

From studying this case, I concluded that motivational tasks are in some ways similar to ambiguous function assignments but are quite different. Task does imply chore and difficulty, whereas assignment is something a person does. However, a motivational/diagnostic task should be relatively easy and even potentially enjoyable. It is not necessarily a test or creator of insight, it is done just to see what happens. It is solely a "yes or no" phenomenon. This could be an alternate explanation for the climbing Squaw Peak exercise for the psychiatrist and his wife. The same could be said for Len and Helen. It was a chore for them to have an outing, much less discuss or resolve meaningful issues. Let us return to our list one last time. We have taken care of mountains, hammers, and treats. Clips and restaurants are left!

Clips

A 20-year-old man was referred to me by his mother, a former patient. The young man was not doing well in college and generally was manipulative, lazy, and in many ways a not-so-slick psychopath. The family was fairly wealthy and so money always seemed to come his way. There were questions of appropriate independence, lying, going to law school, poor relationships, gambling, spending sprees, and more. He liked to talk and gossip in therapy and was quite entertaining. He continually raised questions about his personal "sincerity" regarding anything.

Progress was not being made, so I decided to change course. I asked him to do the three-jar task. He did not. He begged for a second chance. He again did not do the assignment. I raised the question, "Do you think I was dumb enough, at least the second time around, to believe that you would do the assignment?" He said he did not but asked for reconsideration. He was good with words. I specifically assigned a "sincerity task." The task was to carry around a piece of paper in his wallet that said "Sincerely yours" with his name signed and a paper clip attached. He indicated he did have paper clips, a pen, paper, and a wallet. He was told to call me in three weeks. When the call came, he said he had not found the time for the task. It would have taken a moment. In the conversation, I questioned his "sincerity." He was told to contact me if he ever decided to change his ways. He indicated he really did not want to change but just wanted to know "Why!?" I knew he did not think much of his mother, and said, "Because of what you saw your mother and father do in bed one night, and you want to kill him to be her lover." He questioned that, but I told him that he could verify that in any book on psychoanalysis. He then recalled from his study of psychology such an explanation.

I never heard from him again, but his mother called once and indicated that her son was being nicer than usual to her but had not changed his ways. It was clear the patient was not motivated for change per se, but an additional paradoxical method and "negative reframe" seemed to have resulted in some change.

Restaurants: Food for Thought

A couple was referred for marital counseling by another couple, who claimed that I "was the only one who could save a crumbled marriage." Both Jim and Eileen were 28 years old. They had been married for nine years and had two children, ages three and five. He owned a music store and she worked as an interior designer. She was also his bookkeeper. They had been separated for a few months. When we met, I quickly noted he was passive, quite genteel, socially adept, and pleasant. In contrast, she was aggressive, outspoken, forceful, and somewhat domineering. The conversation opened with Eileen's rage and hostility toward Jim's dependent and parasitic ways, which she had apparently tolerated long enough. There was little agreement regarding anything, and it seemed impossible to negotiate a truce long enough to even begin therapy. I asked them both, "Would you do anything to save your marriage?" He said, "Of course." She screamed, "No, he has got to get used to the idea that he is now the father of my children and nothing more. Sometimes I may want him to babysit, when I can't find a sitter, when I go out with my boyfriend, but that is all!" To me it seemed really quite cut and dried, but Jim said, "I feel her position is softening; do you see it?" (This was the first time anyone had ever said no to my question. Many times I have thought people said yes out of politeness, to save face, to say they gave it a last try. But this time this was not the case. I decided we would give it one try.)

I asked Eileen to wander into the music store and let him "pick her up." This was actually how they first met many years ago when he was working in, rather than the owner of, a music store. I told her to accept. I told them to go to an Italian restaurant with average food and no atmosphere. When that was done they should call me and we would determine if another appointment was needed. Jim called later that day and said that they had not had their lunch yet but they did go to a nearby wooded area. They walked and talked. A week later Jim called and said they had not yet had lunch. For that matter, she had not been to the store. A month later the story was the same. Interestingly enough, she resigned as his bookkeeper so she would not have to go to his store. After about three months Jim called and said, "It [the lunch] hasn't happened. It [the marriage] looks like it's over."

There were two purposes here. One was assessment. They both liked Italian food and ate lunch together even after their separation. The second was my hope that they would interact and perhaps communicate in a civil way in a public place. The undone assignment seemed to make real for Jim what had been words, concepts, and the abstract. Thus, it demonstrated not to me, but to him, that Eileen was not motivated for marital counseling and, more important, had no intention of a reconciliation.

Task Construction

Motivational Assessment Tasks

Based upon the above discussion, a motivational assessment task should be constructed as follows:

1. A special task or act should be assigned. The task should be simple, take little physical effort or time, and be potentially enjoyable, tolerable, or at least not distasteful.
2. The task should be "small," "doable," and require very little, if any, financial, energy, and time expenditure. Together with point 1, we emphasize that there should be no reason why the client(s) would not be able to do the task. The task should not have any aspect that is objectionable.
3. The task should be "active" rather than "passive."

4. When more than one person is actively engaged in therapy, the "whole" group or "target" group should be engaged in conducting the task.
5. The task should be delivered with some expectancy.
6. There will be one of two outcomes: either the task will not be done, or it will be done. With the former outcome one would potentially conclude that there is little motivation for treatment, or that the task for some reason had been difficult. Therefore, a second, but easier, motivation task should be given. If there is resistance it needs to be tackled. The quality or accuracy of doing the task is generally unimportant; it is either done or not. If the task is completed per the instructions, then follow the procedure outlined for debriefing when using ambiguous function assignments.
7. If the task is not completed, you can either assume there is no motivation for therapy and terminate, or you can follow the debriefing procedure for ambiguous function assignments and attempt to derive some "therapeutic value" from the exercise.
8. It is best not to call this or any other task a task. That employs hard work and perfection. Calling it an assignment, "home-play" (not work), "an experiment," or the like creates a much more positive approach. It also allows for some flexibility on the part of the client(s).

Ambiguous Function Assignments

According to Lankton and Lankton (1984, 1986), the construction of an ambiguous functioning assignment should include the following (1986, p. 137):

1. A specific task or act is assigned.
2. The purpose of the assignment is not revealed; however, the assignment is given/delivered with the implication and compelling expectancy that much value, learning, and understanding will be derived from the doing and completion of the assignment.
3. An actual physical object is used. Although it is best to use a "neutral" object, symbolic ones can be used. But also remember that just because the therapist thinks it is symbolic does not mean the patient will. If the theory is right, a neutral object will become symbolic.
4. Place binds, or the "illusion of alternatives," on the performance of the task.
5. After the task is completed, maintain "therapeutic leverage" while using the patient's responses by:
   a. Emphasizing and reinforcing each learning

    b. Identifying and accelerating the client's motivation

    c. Not accepting the patient's initial thinking as complete

    d. Continuing the expectancy and implying the existence of more information, meaning, etc.

    e. Challenging or stimulating the client to continued thinking

    f. Directing the client to deeper levels of personal interpretation and meaning

6. Continue the above steps until therapeutic receptivity is maximized and the patient has shown diminishing returns on the activity.

7. There are two possible alternate responses. Either the patient will say he or she got nothing out of doing the assignment, or he or she will not have done the assignment. In either case, follow the points in number five above from the position of "What does that say about you?" "Doing it wrong" can be investigated, and if you wish the person can be given a second choice. Given the illusion of alternatives, the details obtained about the reason for doing things a particular way, picking the object, etc., can be explored, and this may accomplish the anticipated projection. When the task was not done, you can discuss all the reasons that it was not done, what that says about the patient's personality, how it relates to the patient's problems, etc. Depending on your judgement, either the patient can be given a second chance to do the same assignment or you can state, "It is too late now; the learning and the experience just wouldn't be there now." With a certain amount of experience one also becomes aware of those who might not do the assignment correctly, and one can repeat the instructions. One also becomes aware of those who will not follow the directive and can use the paradoxical concept of "You probably won't do this." After the fact at the debriefing one could also say, "Did you really think I thought you would do this thing?"

Although there are great similarities between the two types of tasks, it must be emphasized that a motivational task does not necessarily employ an object or binds. The question is whether or not the individual(s) comply. In contrast, an ambiguous function assignment is meant to be therapeutic regardless of the action(s) taken. In the first case, either therapy continues or therapy is terminated. With an ambiguous function assignment, it is the therapist's task to make the discussion, insight, and experience that follow meaningful to the patient. In a sense, the therapist helps draw out the intended *projection*.

Task Purity and Ambiguity

From the above examples it seems that tasks need not be pure in nature. Tasks can and do overlap categories. They can be ambiguous and skill building simultaneously. There can be a paradoxical element also. The warning is that the patient(s) must be able to handle the various responses at the same time; otherwise the tasks should be constructed more purely and linearly.

What seems to be important is that even what is constructed as an ambiguous task may not really be so ambiguous after all. The context of therapy, the words with which it is presented, may actually focus and narrow the responses.

Tasks can have multiple intents and may have similar pulls for people with similar problems or backgrounds. Of the more than 30 cases in which the jar task was given, almost everyone who had some hypnotic treatment also indicated the jars helped them elicit their own trance. Some without hypnotic treatment but with anxiety symptoms alluded to becoming more relaxed, focused, and at ease. So there may be a common pull based upon some contextual factor, how the task is presented, or something else.

If we consider Haley's (1984) comments about the ordeal of being *in* therapy, for some the ritual, act, assignment may be being in therapy. To take it to an illogical extreme, perhaps therapy, as conducted by some, is nothing more than an ambiguous function assignment. It, however, determines if the patient is motivated. If one is not motivated, all the insight in the world, all the realizations from an ambiguous function assignment will not change the situation. Ultimately, we cannot know what is symbolic for our patients; the point is this technique is a tool, and it is all in how it is presented. Tasks need not and cannot always be pure.

All psychotherapies share at least four effective features (Frank & Frank, 1991): First, an emotionally charged, confiding relationship with a helping person or group; second, a healing setting; third, a rationale, a conceptual scheme or myth that provides a plausible explanation for the patient's symptoms and prescribes a ritual or procedure for resolving them; fourth, a ritual or procedure that requires the active participation of both patient and therapist and is believed by both therapist and patient to be the means of restoring the patient's health. Perhaps an ambiguous function assignment withing the context of treatment is not so ambiguous after all!

There are several rules, however, when using or deciding on any intervention. A therapist must first posit what such an intervention will accomplish. Paradox disrupts the behavioral complex, which may include cognitions and affect. Skill-building assignments develop, build, and re-fine behavioral deficits. Ambiguous function assignments activate patients and develop insights and awareness. Motivational assignments assess therapeutic potential. Although these are loose descriptions of what these actions accomplish, there may be ancillary changes in self-image, family organization, and personal roles. What is important in the use of these assignments is the consideration of what they should accomplish, and what might happen if they did not work. Finally, when considering or using any intervention or task, remember these three simple but important rules:

Know thy patient.

Have a goal.

What have you got to lose if it is well thought out? Something may happen. If you are not reasonably careful, things can get worse.

A New Question

If this were not a psychotherapy paper, what would mountains, ham-mers, jars, treats, and clips all have in common? Perhaps nothing, some-thing, or quite a lot. Ultimately, it might be what you make out of it!

References

Burlingame, H. J. (1974). *History of magic and magicians*. Chicago: Magic Inc.

de Shazer, S. (1985). *Keys to solution in brief therapy*. New York: Norton.

Fisch, R., Weakland, J., & Segal, L. (1982). *The tactics of change: Doing therapy briefly*. San Francisco: Jossey-Bass.

Frank, J. D., & Frank, J. B. (1991). *Persuasion and healing: A comparative study of psychotherapy*. Baltimore: Johns Hopkins.

Frankl, V. (1939). Sur Medikanementosen untrstutzuing der Psychtherapie bei Neursen. *Schweiezer Arshio fur Neurologie und Psychiatrie, 43*, 26–31.

Frankl, V. (1975). Paradoxical intention and dereflection. *Psychotherapy, Theory Research and Practice, 1975, 12*, 226–237.

Gordon, D., & Meyers-Anderson, M. (1981). *Therapeutic patterns of Milton H. Erickson*. Cupertino, CA: Meta Publications.

Haley, J (1973a). *Problem solving therapy*. San Francisco: Jossey-Bass.

Haley, J. (1973b). *Uncommon therapy: The psychiatric techniques of Milton H. Erickson, M.D.* New York: Norton.

Haley, J. (1984). *Ordeal therapy: Unusual ways to change behavior*. San Francisco: Jossey-Bass.

Lankton, S. R. & Lankton, C. H. (1983). *The answer within: The clinical framework of Ericksonian hypnotherapy*. New York: Brunner/Mazel.

Lankton, S. R. & Lankton, C. H. (1984). Personal communication.

Lankton, S. R. & Lankton, C. H. (1986). *Enchantment and intervention in family therapy: Training in Ericksonian approaches.* New York: Brunner/Mazel.

Madanes, C. (1981). *Strategic family therapy.* San Francisco: Jossey-Bass.

Madanes, C. (1984). *Behind the one-way mirror.* San Francisco: Jossey-Bass.

Nelms, H. (1969). *Magic and showmanship: A handbook for conjurers.* New York: Dover.

O'Hanlon, W. H. (1987). *Taproots: Underlying principles of Milton Erickson's therapy and hypnosis.* New York: Norton.

O'Hanlon, W. H., & Hexum, A. L. (1990). *An uncommon casebook: The complete clinical work of Milton H. Erickson, M.D.* New York: Norton.

Palazzoli, M. S., Boscolo, L., Cecchin, G., & Prata, G. (1978). *Paradox and counterparadox.* New York: Jason Aronson.

van der Hart, O. (1981). *Rituals in psychotherapy: Transition and continuity.* New York: Irvington.

Weeks, G. R. (1982). *Paradoxical psychotherapy: Theory and practice with individuals, couples and families.* New York: Brunner/Mazel.

Weiss, M. F. (1992). *Therapeutic secrets, magic, and miracles: The essence of psychotherapy.* Unpublished manuscript.

Zeig, J. K. (1980). *A teaching seminar with Milton H. Erickson M.D.* New York: Brunner/Mazel.

The "February Man" Technique: Successful Replications

Dawn M. White, Ph.D.

Erickson's "February Man" is a revolutionary 1945 case study of the creation of a benign figure in the consciousness of a depressed, fearful young woman. This approach provides for the experiencing of benevolent attention and nurturance that may have been deficient in the formative years. Such deficiencies may cause developmental lags, inexplicable emotional constriction, and fearfulness. This chapter describes two recent case studies patterned after the "February Man" approach. The first case concerns a young man who requested help to stop drinking and sort out relationship and career issues; the second follows a Vietnam veteran grappling with issues of self-worth and suicidal ideation.

My introduction to the "February Man" occurred in 1976 during my initial reading of *Uncommon Therapy* (Haley, 1973). Haley's work provided the foundation for my studies with Erickson over a 4-year period, including his presence on my dissertation committee. I was in a year-long group therapy training in Ann Arbor, Michigan. My presentation to the group was on Erickson's "February Man" approach to working with early issues. It seemed a viable alternative to the arduous and time-consuming methods in use at the time. I wondered whether it was necessary to go over and over negative and traumatic material in the history of a client. It seemed to me that in a fair number of cases such methods only served to make the events larger than life. Shouldn't psychotherapy help to release the hold of traumatic memories rather than reinforce them?

The possibility of relieving areas of neglect, deprivation, and abuse with befriending attention, positive regard, pleasant conservation, developmentally appropriate instruction, and guidance seemed a revolutionary way

Address correspondence to Dawn M. White, Ph.D., P.O. Box 73, Cornville, AZ 86325.

to provide a "child" with "quality time" after the fact. The long-suffering client could relax, participate, and change effectively and relatively painlessly without the need for vilifying or confronting relatives and caretakers, as is in fashion even today. Rather, he or she would be provided the opportunity to interact with a benign and benevolent figure who supplied the equivalent of unconditional love. The most temporally and situationally efficient therapeutic process for an individual is an intrapsychic one. This is indeed the advantage of using Erickson's "February Man" approach.

When one peruses the narrative contained in *Uncommon Therapy* (Haley, 1973) and the complete transcript in *The February Man* (Erickson & Rossi, 1989), it is interesting to note the differences between the verbatim record contained in the latter and the blend of amnesia and selective memory in Erickson's didactic narrative to Haley. Is the most effective therapy done in trance, and the risk of amnesia for details a possible side effect? Busy clinicians with no immediate access to their notes often will confuse details of history, dates and times, and the like. Yet when face to face with the client, the essence of the client's experience as well as historical details become immediately accessible.

A stenographer was not present at the client's first session with Erickson. One might speculate that the first session involved the gathering of history and other diagnostic information, assessing responsiveness and preparing the ground for the seeding of ideas in the later sessions. During my visits with Erickson (1976 to 1980), I observed that he worked with clients and students in much the same way: bantering, trading puns, asking questions, and making comments that did not immediately seem related. This behavior fixated attention, created confusion, stimulated mental searches, induced trance, and promoted healing while he was simultaneously sizing up the student/client through his observation of verbal and nonverbal behavior. No standard hypnotizability tests! Instead, he would launch into gleaning pertinent history, depotentiating resistance, reframing and healing troublesome or traumatic memories, and enlarging the patient's understanding of conscious limitations versus the limitless potential of unconscious wisdom.

Erickson's complete "February Man" therapy consisted of the previously mentioned unrecorded session followed by four lengthy psychotherapy sessions that took place in 1945. The "February Man" character is introduced in the second part of the first recorded session.

Erickson begins by building feelings of safety and trust for a person that the patient will be talking with and spending time with in the future: "But somehow or other you will realize that you are safe, that you are secure, that there is somebody you know and can trust and whom you can recognize who will be with you, with whom you can talk and with whom you can shake hands" (p. 31) . He regresses her by stimulating a search for the first time she shook hands and then asks, "Do you suppose you know what month it is right now? She said, "February," although the session took place in March. He then continues to use a gentle, persuasive manner of speaking, as an adult might talk with a small child. He is thus falling into the role of that "somebody you know and can trust, who will be with you, with whom you can talk" (p. 31). He reassures her that she is going to see him again and asks her questions that pertain to her future. "What do you think you will be when you grow up? Do you think you will have to work hard? Is there anything you don't like and understand?" She reveals the most troublesome question: "Where did Daddy go when he died?" (p. 38). Erickson is very careful in pointing out that the explanation he gives is for a little girl's understanding and that as she grows older she will have an expanded understanding of this matter.

In the next visit Erickson affirms that all the visits have been in February and asks her a rhetorical question: "What are you going to call me? The February Man?" (p. 63). She says "Sure," and he reminds her that he had told her he would see her again a long time ago. She remembers. Later they talk about her caring aunt and uncle, and lessons are drawn regarding life. He uses the aunt and uncle to underscore the importance of children growing up with happy memories of their caretakers. The "February Man" also is experienced as warm and supportive. Her unconscious memory is incorporating the warmth and wisdom of the "February Man" (p. 65). In discussion of this section Rossi hypothesizes that "these memories will become the basis of her future self-esteem and confidence in raising her own children" (p. 65).

The foregoing is only an introduction to Erickson's "February Man" approach. The text is a fascinating and detailed guide for the clinician interested in using this potent and revolutionary psychotherapeutic tool. This approach to psychotherapy pioneered in 1945 may well remain "state of the art" into the 21st century.

What follows is the description and discussion of two cases. The first case predates my reading of the verbatim script and discussion as presented in Erickson and Rossi's book. In the second case I did refer to the script, yet I do not think one treatment was more successful than the other.

In both cases I stayed with taking the name of the therapeutic figure from the months of the year. In other cases not mentioned here I used names borrowed from literature or made up to suit the personality of the character and the inclinations of the client.

In the second case the therapeutic figure started out as female, a second male character was introduced at the patient's request, and I later introduced a third character as necessary for the termination of therapy. I hoped that this evolution reinforced the client's awareness of many sources of teaching and support. I am unsure whether the literary figure is as powerful as the "February Man" prototype.

The "February Man": A Variation on the Theme

My first case involves a client who will be referred to as John. He was born in February in the latter part of the sixties. He began therapy at age 22 and continued a pattern of weekly, biweekly, and monthly sessions for about 15 months. His presenting problem was episodic alcohol abuse. He had tried to stop on his own unsuccessfully. He drank about 12 beers a night at home. He didn't want to join AA or inpatient programs. I asked him why he wanted to stop drinking. He said he wanted to feel healthy; he didn't want to feel awful anymore the morning after a drinking episode.

At age 14 he lived with his maternal grandmother, who drank heavily. She was lonely, a nocturnal wine drinker, and on one occasion she got so drunk she fell and hurt her head.

John's father died at age 45 when John was only two years old. His mother never remarried. He had a half brother, nine years older than he, who had a drinking problem. His sister, three years older, was away in college.

John revealed that he started drinking at age 15 shortly after he stopped living with the alcoholic grandmother. His pattern was to drink on weekends. He said the drinking was a problem in his relationships with girlfriends. John wanted help to stop drinking and to sort out some issues regarding his job and training for the future. He aspired to a degree in mechanical engineering but was ambivalent about giving up his job. He returned for hypnotherapy two weeks later.

He had stayed away from alcohol for more than a week when he had a six-pack of beer and drank every night thereafter. On the weekend he got "really drunk." He didn't sleep well and had a hangover all day. He then drank one more beer. I concentrated on working on self-esteem. He responded well to hypnosis, achieving a medium trance. I also helped him start searches regarding his 4-month relationship with his girlfriend, slipping in metaphors addressing the drinking problem, including the following story:

Once upon a time a friend of mine bought a beautiful *Ficus benjamina*, more commonly known as a weeping fig. He was an amateur botanist and had a large number of different plants in and around his house. He knew this plant was capable of becoming a tree, given the right conditions. He nurtured and cherished the young plant with its glossy oval leaves and busy network of twiggy brown branches. He gave it just the right amount of sun and just the right amount of water, occasionally laced with plant food. It grew into a graceful presence in just a few years. The leaves tapered tenderly, with glossy smooth surfaces facing the sun. If you accidentally broke off a leaf or twig, it would weep milky tears.

One summer my friend took a trip to Alaska. A neighbor offered to water the plants and watch the house. My friend returned after a month, having thoroughly enjoyed his vacation and looking forward to seeing his plants. He was deeply disturbed at what he found. His well-meaning friend had overwatered so many plants that he had watered them to death. My friend spent the day disposing of dead plants and drying out soggy soil. He was thus able to save some, but not his *Ficus benjamina*. Its dead brown leaves carpeted the pot and the floor around it, and all that remained was a twiggy skeleton.

Now I've often wondered how much liquid is necessary for good health. Would cool, pure water be all the body needs? What of the liquids contained in gravies, soups, juices, vegetables, and fruit? What about coffee and tea? Is it really necessary or healthy to drink cow's milk? How important is mother's milk, in infancy, and how long should breast feeding proceed? Is it true that breastfed babies are healthy, content, immunologically advantaged? Why is alcohol harmful to lesser or greater degrees and yet is used medicinally with good results? Why do some people become problem drinkers who lose jobs, wreck relationships, and ruin their health? Why would anyone want to drink to excess? Why would anyone want to quit?

John returned two weeks later. He hadn't drunk even though he'd been "all stressed out" early in the week about his relationship with his girlfriend. He said he had tried not to be insecure with anybody, including his girlfriend. In session three we explored early memories in and out of trance. He remembered coming home along with his sister to a silent, empty house. He called himself a "latchkey kid." His only memory of his father was of Mom and Dad going in the bedroom and Mom emerging with a bloody nose. "No one in the family talks about Dad. He was a physicist who died of a heart attack at 45." In trance work I evoked the memory of Mom and Dad fighting and provided empowering possibilities that would help diffuse the sad and helpless feelings. I used stories of Luke Skywalker and his apprenticeship with Yoda from the *Star Wars* Trilogy, moving him into the future to the discovery of new strengths. The childhood memories made him teary. Upon awakening he said he now realized how much of an impact those occurrences must have had on him at age two. He was amazed he could remember himself at two years of age.

During session four, John wanted to work on feelings of insecurity and jealousy regarding his girlfriend. We discussed his Myers Briggs Type Inventory (MBTI) profile as a preliminary to the hypnotic work. (I sometimes use the MBTI in working with couples, as a way of helping them understand and change the way they perceive themselves and each other.)

At his next session John reported having fallen off the wagon. He had become very depressed about himself, crying in front of his mother, from whom he rented a room. Among others, I used a story from *Journey to Ixtlan* (Castaneda, 1972, p. 8). In the story the medicine man Don Juan confesses to having been a drunk in his youth. He states he just decided to quit drinking one day, and simply followed through on that resolution.

At his sixth session John reported sobriety since the previous session, and we worked on sorting through issues regarding schooling and work. The next two sessions involved work on his relationship with his mother and his girlfriend. I used a story that illustrated the need for space and freedom within loving relationships. John's girlfriend was present for session nine. We worked on the relationship using the MBTI and focusing on positives, including memories of first falling in love.

At his 10th session John announced his decision to move out of his mother's house despite nagging feelings of guilt. He reported having disagreements with his girlfriend, although they had decided to live together. In trance work I used a story about a man taking flying lessons as a foundation and preparation for his solo flight.

John's life seemed full of turbulence for the next two months although he did not go back to drinking. Sessions 11, 12, and 13 were therefore oriented toward stress reduction and sorting through doubts about the relationship with his now live-in girlfriend, insecurities about his job situation, and worries about college plans. He had been sober since March 13, the end of his only relapse. It was now June 4. I decided on drastic action that I hoped would have a deep and lasting therapeutic impact. Enter the "February Man."

I regressed John to his birthday in February, in his kindergarten year. He said he was walking along the wall in kindergarten.

> "It's my birthday, I'm by myself. I'm feeling okay, not happy, not sad. My family knows it is my birthday, my friends don't know. My mother cuts my hair very short. The kids make fun of my haircut."
> "Do you know that tall, friendly man standing by the door?"
> "No."

"Take a good look. You have met him before and you are looking forward to many happy visits. I wonder if he knows it's your birthday. Go ahead and tell him, if you'd like. He's awfully tall, isn't he? He wants to shake your hand and wish you a happy birthday. He wants to know if you remember him. What would you like to say to him?"

Silence.

"I wonder where you will see him again."

This was the first time I used this technique. My treatment plan notes read:

He needs a father figure. Need to tailor each encounter to his history. Keep it loose. Have the "February Man" emphasize and appreciate his uniqueness, remind him he's one of a kind. Keep in mind that his earliest conscious memory is age seven. Need to fill in first seven years. Have the "February Man" visit during those years.

Session 15 was partly devoted to some necessary work for the prevention of migraines. John was then regressed to two years of age to the memory of Dad's raised voice in the bedroom and Mom emerging with a bloody nose. He looked scared and little. I talked about little John needing to be held and comforted. How safe and secure it would feel to be warm and loved and protected, and that might give him the strength to comfort himself, maybe even send comforting thoughts to his mother. Once again there were tears. "That really felt sad and scary, didn't it? I'm sorry. It's mostly better now, isn't it? I have a nice surprise for you. What do you think is going to happen on your next birthday? You are going to meet someone who wants to meet you. I think you are going to like him a lot. You can tell him anything you want. You know you are going to be bigger, you are going to be three years old!"

I then took him forward to his third birthday and his first chronological meeting with the "February Man."

"Isn't he tall? He's smiling at you 'cause he likes little kids, he especially likes you. What do you want to ask him?"

"Where have you been?" This was said in a tone of wonder, and I imagined it might have been followed by, "I've been waiting and waiting. It's about time you showed up."

"I've been far away, but I've been thinking about you, wondering how you've been doing. Hoping you were safe and growing and smiling every day." I asked John what he was wearing. He said he was wearing a striped shirt and red pants. I asked him where he was.

"I'm kneeling on a chair."

"He's coming closer, isn't he? He's bending down to pick you up. Way up! And doesn't it feel good to be up so high? You can see everything. Now he is sitting down on the sofa and you get to sit on his lap. That's pretty high up too, isn't it? He sure likes you a lot. He knows you are cute and cuddly. Doesn't it feel good to be hugged, to feel safe and warm and special. He knows that there's no one in the whole world just like you. You are the only John David Bates. He likes you just for being you. You really don't want to talk, do you? It just feels so good and so warm. He wants to be quiet too. He just wants to hold you and cuddle up, so go ahead and enjoy cuddling as long as you want."

After pausing almost a minute, I said: "The 'February Man' has to leave now, John. You don't want him to leave, do you? He wants to come back and see you next year. Do you know you will be four then? He wants to see how much you will grow while he is gone. Do you think you will grow?" He nodded very slowly.

At his 16th session John was regressed to his birthday at age four. The "February Man" gave him lots of positive feedback about how nicely he had grown, and lots of unconditional acceptance."Do you know that you are the only person in the whole world exactly like you? There's only one of you with that dark curly hair and that special voice. I bet you can sing real loud. Do you know there's no one who walks just like you? That's right. Did you ever see the way a cat walks? You don't walk like that, do you? It would be fun to walk like a cat, wouldn't it? But right now you can enjoy walking like John David Bates." I hoped that these words would stimulate a sense of happy self-acceptance. Toward the end of trance I asked if he had any questions.

"Why does he have to go?" he said in a plaintive tone.

"I don't know, but I do know that he wouldn't miss seeing you again for anything."

Upon awakening John remarked that he hadn't really remembered himself on his fourth birthday. He hadn't remembered what he wore or anything. He just knew it was his fourth birthday and felt good. He asked, "Why does he have to be back in a year? A year is so long."

"Perhaps he'll be back sooner than you expect," I answered.

At his next session, therefore, I broke tradition and regressed John to the fourth of July. He was now almost 4½ years old. I asked him where he was.

"I'm on his shoulder, watching fireworks."

The "February Man" then related stories from his travels. He had been on a ship along the coast of Alaska and had seen many wonderful things. He said he had missed John so he had hurried back early.

After the fireworks, John was told he was getting very sleepy, so the "February Man" carried him back to his room and tucked him in with "Good night, sleep tight. Sleep snug as a bug in a rug, a little warm sleepy bug in a rug." The whisper of a smile appeared on John's face.

At his next session, John affirmed that he was still sober but that he sometimes felt his girlfriend was unwittingly sabotaging his sobriety. For instance, she kept beer in the house. He realized that problems with his girlfriend and stress at work were fairly routine occurrences. He did think that things were improving since I had referred her for individual therapy with a colleague. John continued to plan for the day when he would quit work and pursue his engineering degree.

This time, although interspersed "February Man" references were made, I concentrated on a story, "The Boy Who Lost His Way" (Wallace, 1985). I did not use the name "February Man" but wove his persona into the story at strategic places so that there were feelings of support and goodwill permeating from a guardian angel–like presence, as the boy in the story overcame one obstacle after another.

John's 20th session was also his last "February Man" session. In retrospect, I believe that the reason I suspended the "February Man" work was that there were urgent relationship issues that needed to be addressed. There also remained issues of emancipation from his mother, stress at work, a decision to quit smoking, and the reinforcement of his continued sobriety.

The final "February Man" session began with a discussion of John's recognition that his migraines were largely stress related. He hadn't had any headaches during his two week vacation. In contrast, he had already had a couple since returning to work.

After trance induction, John regressed to five years old on his birthday. He was in a restaurant with his mother, brother, sister, and grandmother. He nodded yes to my comment, "I bet you are hungry."

"Yes, I think I'll have spaghetti and chocolate cake."

When he got back home, the "February Man" was waiting on the sofa. When I asked John where he was, he said he was kneeling on a chair looking out the window. He wanted to go out front and play in the snow. They decided to build a snowman, but it turned into a snow woman. They found weeds for hair. A piece of red cloth was the mouth, a stick made a nose, and pebbles were used for eyes. This was John's description of what went on outside. I asked questions that helped to reinforce comfort, curiosity, excitement, camaraderie.

After coming out of trance John was amnesic for most of the session. He asked me if it was okay to think about drinking. I told him stories of successfully sober clients who were now on their second year and tenth year of sobriety, respectively. I mentioned that they both thought about drinking but continued to be sober. I asked him what happened when I asked him not to think about chocolate cake. He nodded in recognition of the point. He said he was meeting a friend who was an alcoholic. I wondered if he could just tell him he had decided to quit. With signs of relief he said he would and smiled, "Thanks, Dawn."

John and his girlfriend came in for the next session, obviously tense. They had been fighting. For the last 20 minutes I hypnotized John for stress reduction and his part in the dysfunctional relationship equation. This was partly because I wanted John to have some time alone for individual work, to underscore my commitment to his therapy.

A month later I provided more reinforcement for sobriety: mostly direct suggestion cataloging how much he had accomplished. More work was also done regarding his relationship with his girlfriend and paranoid feelings about his boss. He achieved a deeper trance than he had in some time and seemed to enjoy the stories chosen, particularly a script entitled "A Quiet Birth" from *Hypnotherapy Scripts* (Havens & Walters, 1989). Later he asked if he might ever drink again. I said I didn't know but that he might find he didn't like it if he did.

A quit-smoking session was next. Complete smoking cessation was achieved at his second session about a month later. He had to quit therapy for a time for financial reasons but said his girlfriend wanted counseling for their upcoming marriage. I looked forward to the opportunity of following Erickson's script more closely, given the similar dynamics involved. However, in the next few months John accomplished quitting his job and moving to the engineering school location. He spoke with me by phone twice, mainly about settling his bill. He sounded fine and said they were doing well and that his girlfriend would also be entering engineering school when they could afford tuition.

The December Lady, the January Man, and Vasudeva

Dave was born in August in the mid-forties. He had a high IQ and was widely read. He had suicidal proclivities and a strong need to control his own destiny. He was grappling with problems of self-worth in his family life and work. He had enlisted in the army after high school and served two tours in Vietnam. He left because of a "reduction in force." He reported having suicidal ideation in Vietnam. "I re-enlisted to the furthest outpost, didn't want to come back." Suicidal ideation was a consistent issue, with much rumination about death and the meaning of life.

Dave was 18 months old when his home burned to the ground. His mother died in the fire. He did not talk much about his father except to say they did not get along until after he was grown. He felt he had no role models. Dave had two older sisters. He frequently felt isolated, although he did well academically and excelled in sports.

Dave described several highly traumatic incidents in Vietnam. He said his second marriage had deteriorated to being "in name only." He worked at substitute teaching, was a trapper and an occasional blacksmith.

Five years prior, Dave's wife had attempted suicide. "I've done everything in the world to break up my marriage," he reported, "It would have been healthier for her to get a divorce. I would have gone off to Alaska trapping and disappeared."

Dave was an extremely challenging client. He would often get in the way of his own therapy, intellectualizing his own feelings and those of significant others. I sometimes had the feeling he kept one eye open during hypnotherapy. His pattern of obsessive analysis of books, life, and therapy needed to be regularly disrupted while one gently provided alternate routes for the maintenance of equilibrium. Concentration on insight was discouraged in favor of acceptance of feeling and functioning better with his family and his work. Once we achieved a deep level of healing of childhood and Vietnam-related issues, it was hoped, his suicidal ideation would abate.

Dave responded well and felt much relief at the end of each session. He was glad that I was able to keep him off balance because he felt he had controlled previous therapists.

Greatly challenged, I began what Rossi calls "the evolving of consciousness and identity" (Erickson & Rossi, 1989) by introducing a character called the "December Lady." They met in early December at his grandmother's boarding house. I chose a female, figuring that his mother's early death must have resulted in considerable maternal deprivation. Dave, however, had other ideas. Upon awakening he informed me that a female would not work for him. He had disliked his grandmother intensely.

At the next session I again introduced the "December Lady." This time her husband was in tow and Dave got to spend time with him, because the woman had errands to run. They spent time outdoors, discussed carpentry, and the man promised to teach him how to make something he would enjoy very much.

In all the work of this type I have not assumed the role of the therapeutic character the way Erickson did. Instead, I describe the surrogate figure and together we fill in details of the interaction according to the client's history and therapeutic needs.

After the introduction of the "January Man," Dave enjoyed many visits, during which they would involve themselves in carpentry projects. The early work was aimed at healing the loss of his mother. The "December Lady" would tweak his nose gently and tell him how cute and lovable he was. She would hold his hand and walk with him. When they stopped to rest on a bench, she would invite him to climb onto her lap. He hesitated although he said she smelled good, like bread and perfume. She picked him up and cuddled him against her. After he stopped pushing away, it did feel good. I added interpretations such as "She likes you just for being you. She thinks you are very cute and lovable." Months later he announced that the lady liked him just for being him, but she was "just a lady."

In January she introduced him to her husband. Thus he got to spend quality time with a man he could admire. The "January Man" told him of his younger days as a carpenter and about the many wonderful and useful things he had made. He asked him if he would like to learn to make something. I came up with the idea of a small bench, which he could carry around and sit on whenever he wanted, but Dave changed the project into the making of a box into which he could put his treasured objects. Each time he met the "January Man" I had him ask questions and make conversation. I would let him tell me what the man said or provide answers through narration. "He likes being with you and especially likes to help you make things."

At one session I had him discuss with the "January Man" what he had heard about Dave's mother, how sorry he was that she had died. He had known her as a little girl and later when she grew up. He talked about fire, about matches, candles, fireplaces, and how hard it was to put out a fire once it got out of control. He was glad the rest of the family survived and he had gotten to meet little Dave. He said that sometimes when bad things happen to people they feel really bad about it, like it was their fault. "You were so little, it was not your fault. Isn't it good to know it was not your fault? You just needed lots of hugging 'cause you missed your mother. I wonder if you cried a lot or were afraid to cry and just felt alone and scared. Do you remember how you felt?" A lone tear appeared. "I wish I had been there to hold you and keep you safe. You can make believe I was. Isn't it nice to know that I can do that now?"

Within six months Dave noticed a freeing up of his emotions. "I think I have been numb all my life. Now I can feel sadness. I have been able to cry in therapy and at home." At one point he said the "January Man" had become an image with an emotion. I didn't ask what he meant by that because of his tendency to intellectualize. I just accepted his statement with a nod. Toward the end of therapy he said that the "January Man" was now perceived consciously as the ultimate grandfather, and all of his ancestors. He said he liked being active in a physical way in their time spent together.

In our last two sessions I utilized the character Vasudeva from *Siddhartha* (Hesse,1951). I chose *Siddhartha* for a number of reasons. Dave had read and enjoyed the book. Toward the end of therapy his wife had asked for a divorce, and it had become final with mutual consent. With the dissolution of his marriage he was essentially without a home. These issues, along with the pain of letting go of offspring, were also found in the Siddhartha story. Dave had to agree to his wife's having custody of their two sons. Their house was going on the market, and she was taking a new job in another town. With the ending of therapy, I hoped he would have a Vasudeva-like figure in his consciousness. Vasudeva was the personification of the good therapist. In describing him Hesse says, "He felt his troubles, his anxieties and his secret hopes flow across to him and return again. Disclosing his wound to this listener was the same as bathing it in the river, until it became cool and one with the river" (p.133). The river seemed the perfect symbol of cleansing, moving on, flowing freely; the river was ever new.

True to character, Dave analyzed most aspects of his therapy. Besides the freeing up of emotion noted earlier, he had a number of observations:

- He had cut down on smoking without consciously wanting to or trying.
- His 20- to 30-cup coffee habit was down to almost nothing.
- His blood pressure had improved.
- In his substitute teaching, his attitudes to his students had changed so that he really looked forward to assignments. He was apparently often in trance when teaching, as he was frequently unaware of his back and leg pain until the end of the school day.
- He didn't feel scattered anymore and was acutely aware of the difference.
- He felt quieter and more hopeful
- He was losing his obsession with dying. "I want to be alive next year. I have a right to be here."

- "One of my cries has been I haven't had a mother. Not so. I have a mother, she's just not here. That's a whole different concept."
- "I'm not railing against the divorce, the situation with Susan and about my kids, the custody arrangement." He said he hadn't become a basket case when his wife asked for a divorce although he felt that way briefly when it occurred. At previous times of being on the brink of divorce he had felt compelled to control his wife and the situation, something she had bitterly resented. He had on those occasions succeeded in aborting and postponing the inevitable.
- In summary he said, "The things that we have done have been incredibly beneficial, and the most important part has been spiritual." I believe he was referring here to what Rossi calls the "evolution of consciousness" (Erickson & Rossi, 1989).

Summary

The first part of this chapter referenced the original "February Man" work done in 1945 by Milton Erickson. Those of us who knew him and observed his work in the decade before his death at age 79 are no doubt surprised that he had already mastered indirect approaches in 1945 while still in his mid-forties.

The second part of this chapter provided a fairly detailed account of "February Man" work in the context of Ericksonian therapy done weekly, biweekly, or monthly over a 14-month period. The client was in his early twenties. He requested help to quit drinking and to sort out relationship and vocational issues.

The third section described another (abbreviated) example of "February Man" work. It outlines work done with a Vietnam veteran in his mid-forties grappling with issues of self-worth and suicidal ideation. I felt it important to provide at least one example that detailed the progress of therapy inclusive of some actual dialogue. This section on the other hand is considerably more abbreviated.

In his foreword to "The February Man," Sidney Rosen says, "I was excited by the idea that this appeared to be the first instance in which a therapist had actually changed the history of a patient." He went on to say that his new understanding of it involves the expansion of awareness in the present, not the past.

This is also my own understanding. This work does not involve changing actual history. It may not be much different from the benefits that accrue when one is absorbed in the characters and story line of a book that provides therapeutic parallels. How many of us have identified deeply with the stories woven into our own lives by spiritual leaders or stories told skillfully by teachers, parents, strangers that moved us to indignation, joy, or compassion. It is important, however, to understand that there is a difference. There is more to the "February Man" approach. It is more personal, more interactive, more tailored to a particular history. Its potential for enriching a client's experience, for easing the pain of early neglect, for providing for quality time with an adult, and for relaxing the hold of traumatic events is exciting and promising. Being "Ericksonian" means being flexible, holistic, fluid. It would be difficult to pinpoint cause and effect in the two cases presented. The "February Man" work was not done in a vacuum but in conjunction with other Ericksonian approaches. Perhaps what really matters is the fact that in each case the individual client was served well.

References

Castaneda, C. (1972). *Journey to Ixtlan*. New York: Simon & Schuster.

Erickson, M. H., & Rossi, E. L. (1989). *The February man*. New York: Brunner/ Mazel.

Haley, J. (1973). *Uncommon therapy*. New York: Norton.

Havens, R. A., & Walters, C. (1989). *Hypnotherapy scripts*. New York: Brunner/ Mazel.

Hesse, H. (1951). *Siddhartha*. New York: New Directions.

Wallace, L. (1985). *Stories for the third ear*. New York: Norton.

Ericksonian Communication and Hypnotic Strategies in the Management of Tics and Tourette Syndrome in Children and Adolescents

Daniel P. Kohen, M.D.

Tourette syndrome (TS) is a complex neurobehavioral disorder with onset in childhood of multiple motor tics and vocalizations. A common misbelief is that children with TS are unable to exercise control over their vocalizations and movements. Because TS commonly goes undiagnosed for 3 to 5 years, children with TS often experience ostracism and a sense of loss of control over their bodies.

No prospective, systematic studies of hypnosis in the management of TS have been found in the literature. Several clinical investigators have described the successful application of self-regulatory techniques for the amelioration of symptoms of TS. This report describes the clinically effective, Ericksonian-inspired approach we have utilized during the past 13 years to assist young people with this complex disorder in helping themselves.

Introduction

Description of Syndrome

Tourette syndrome (TS) is a complex, hereditary neurobehavioral disorder characterized by a constellation of troubling symptoms and defined

Address correspondence to Daniel P. Kohen, M.D., Behavioral Pediatrics Program, University of Minnesota, Suite 100—University Office Plaza, 2221 University Ave. S.E., Minneapolis, MN 55414.

by the onset in childhood of multiple motor tics and vocalizations present almost daily for at least one year (American Psychiatric Association, 1994). Associated behaviors and symptoms may include attention deficit disorder with or without hyperactivity, learning and conduct disorders, obsessive-compulsive phenomena, echo or copying behaviors, and coprolalia (inappropriate uttering of obscenities). It is commonly believed that children with TS are "unable to control themselves" with regard to their troublesome spontaneous movements and vocalizations, and these behaviors are, accordingly, typically thought of, and referred to, as involuntary.

Whereas TS was thought of in the past as a disorder of low incidence, it has recently come to be understood as hereditary and common (Comings, 1990; Comings, Comings, & Knell, 1989). Reports vary from a prevalence of 4 to 5 per 10,000 children to up to 1 in 100 school-aged boys (Comings, 1990; American Psychiatric Association, 1994).

Three times as common in boys as in girls, it is said to affect as many as a million Americans. The syndrome is believed to be caused by an overabundance of dopamine, the central nervous system chemical said to control movement.

The impact of TS on a child's (and family's) psychological, emotional, and social growth can be devastating. The central symptoms of TS, irregular and unpredictable stereotyped movements (tics) of the face, hands, and body, and "uncontrolled" vocalizations that may include bleating, whistling, barking, snorting, or sniffing sounds, or obscenities, typically expose these young people to considerable social ridicule and rejection, both within their families and in peer groups at home and school.

Typically, children develop TS between the ages of 2 and 15 years, with a mean age at onset of 7 years (Golden, 1986). More important, this condition often goes undiagnosed for 3 to 5 years, during which time children with TS may experience social difficulties even including ostracism, and the development of a sense of loss of control over their bodies and their lives. This may result in a long-term reduction in self-esteem, a range of psychological problems, and serious difficulties with relationships.

Treatment Issues

Many reports have described appropriate and successful adjunctive application of hypnotherapeutic techniques (relaxation/mental imagery [RMI]) for a variety of clinical pediatric situations (Gardner & Olness, 1988; Kohen, Olness, Colwell, & Heimel, 1984; Olness, 1975; Young, 1984) asthma (Aronoff, Aronoff, & Peck, 1975; Kohen et al., 1984), migraine headaches (Olness, MacDonald, & Uden, 1987), pelvic examinations (Kohen, 1980), acute pain and anxiety (Kohen et al., 1984), muscle spasm disorders and epilepsy (Young, 1984), and habit disorders (Kohen, 1991), as well as for coping with chronic and terminal illness (Gardner, 1976; Gardner & Olness, 1988). One report on a large series of pediatric patient problems managed with hypnotherapy notes the successful use of RMI among patients with chronic simple tics, but no patients with complex chronic tic disorders were included (Kohen et al., 1984).

The specific uses of relaxation, hypnosis, biofeedback, and analogous self-regulatory techniques for complex tic disorders are rarely mentioned in the literature (Clements, 1972; Friedman, 1980; Tophoff, 1973), and no prospective, controlled, or systematic studies of the value of these techniques for TS have been identified in the literature. Hypnotherapy has been employed in a number of single-case studies, and results have ranged from complete remission (Lindner & Stevens, 1967; Spithill, 1974) to temporary symptom relief (Eisenberg, Ascher, & Kanner, 1959; Fernando, 1967; McKinnon, 1967; Polites, Kruger, & Stevenson, 1965; Schneck, 1960). Some have speculated that successful treatment using these techniques results from changes in physiological arousal during the treatment session (Turpin, 1983). Several anxiety-reduction techniques based on desensitization or relaxation have been described (St. James-Roberts & Powell, 1979; Savicki & Carlin, 1972; Thomas, Abrams, & Johnson, 1971) and there has been limited generalization of benefits (Canavan & Powell, 1981; Turpin & Powell, 1984).

Cue-controlled relaxation techniques also have been used by Turpin and Powell (1984) to encourage generalization. Others have utilized focused relaxation directed toward individual muscle groups involved in tic movements (Bliss, 1980) and response prevention (Bullen & Hemsley, 1984).

More recently, several clinical investigators have described the successful application of self-regulatory (cyberphysiologic) techniques for the management and amelioration of symptoms of TS. So-called habit reversal techniques have been successfully utilized with adolescents and adults with tics (Azrin & Nunn, 1973; Azrin, Nunn, & Frantz, 1980; Finney, Rapoff, Hall, & Christophersen, 1983). Tansey (1986) reported symptom control with sustained tic elimination in a 14-year-old boy with TS through EEG sensorimotor rhythm (SMR) biofeedback training. Kohen and Botts (1987) reported the clinical effectiveness of RMI in four children (5 to 9½ years of age). Zahm (1983) described a carefully done clinical outcome study of hypnosis therapy, and Young and associates (Young, 1989, 1991; Young & Montano, 1988) have recently described their success with a hypnobehavioral approach to helping youngsters with TS to develop effective self-management skills.

For our purposes, we define RMI (equivalent to self-hypnosis) as *an alternative state of consciousness, usually but not always involving relaxation, in which an individual develops heightened concentration on a particular idea or image for the purpose of maximizing some potential or realizing some goal.* Children understand the phenomenon of self-hypnosis as a natural, everyday experience and readily accept RMI as something with which they are familiar, which begins with daydreaming or imagining (Gardner & Olness, 1988), and which is a skill they can learn to cultivate to help themselves.

Although the use of drugs, such as haloperidol (Haldol), is well supported through a series of double-blind drug studies in adults (King & Ollendick, 1984), their use in children with TS is less definitively supported (Golden, 1986) and their side effects more disturbing. Although the symptoms of TS are controllable by medication in 80% of children treated, the medication that is most effective (typically haloperidol or related psychoactive medications) also may cause significant physiological, cognitive, and behavioral side effects, often sufficiently problematic to cause patients and families to spontaneously discontinue medication use. Even some of the so-called lesser side effects (e.g., drowsiness, weight gain, and school avoidance or phobic behavior) are so unacceptable to some that only 20 to 40% of TS patients continue medication for long periods.

Treatment based on or incorporating a self-management approach, such as the cyberphysiologic strategy of relaxation and mental imagery (RMI), adds significantly to the treatment options available to children suffering from TS without increasing their risks of negative side effects. Recently a thorough compendium has been prepared to aid families in the understanding and management of TS (Haerle, 1992). This broad-based parents' guide is promoted as "the first book that families should read." Sadly, however, it includes nothing positive regarding even the potential value of hypnotic or related self-awareness-promoting or self-management strategies. The sole reference to hypnosis is a brief mention of it as something of which the family should beware, and as something commonly and mistakenly portrayed as a "miracle cure." Although discussion abounds on "behavior management," little is directed to self-management, and no reference appears in the index to biofeedback, relaxation, imagery, or related strategies, any or all of which may well be utilized by patients with TS as an adjunct in their overall management.

As of this writing a computer database review of the existing literature reveals no published information on any systematic or prospective controlled studies of hypnotherapeutic applications to TS. A project proposal we have developed currently awaits funding. This project will allow standard pharmacological treatment to be compared to the behavioral intervention of RMI in a prospective and controlled fashion at three institutions in the United States.

Issues in Assessment: the First Visit

The clinical approach and strategies described below have evolved in the context of my clinical outpatient consultative practice in behavioral pediatrics during the past 13 years. An outpatient program based first at a major children's hospital and more recently at a university hospital, the behavioral pediatrics program draws referrals from the broad five-state area of Minnesota, Wisconsin, Iowa, North Dakota, and South Dakota, as well as from the metropolitan Twin Cities community. A diverse group of clinicians regularly refer patients for problems including disorders of elimination (enuresis, encopresis), recurrent somatic complaints (migraine headaches, recurrent abdominal pain), pain (chronic, associated with chronic illness and procedures, etc.), habit disorders (thumb sucking, tics, etc.), behavioral and adjustment problems, and adjustment to chronic illness (cystic fibrosis, kidney disease, cancer). Within this population, referrals for assistance in management of tics or TS have in recent years represented five to seven percent of new patient referrals per year, with, for example, seven such referrals in 1992.

The most important thing the clinician can do to facilitate the possibility of change in a child or adolescent with TS is to first develop a thoughtful, sensitive, and carefully paced rapport in which the child's belief in, and trust of, the clinician is first assured and then becomes pivotal as the communication itself becomes therapeutic. Unless prior experiences with clinicians have been particularly negative, this ought to be relatively easily accomplished early in the relationship, beginning with the first contact.

When I meet children for the first time in the waiting room, I commonly introduce myself directly to them (and not to their parents, as they likely have experienced in the past). Besides being natural and respectful, this approach is designed to implicitly tune in to the child and to what I know they need to have (a sense of personal competence), and in the process *create an atmosphere of curiosity and positive expectancy*. Thus, if a child is used to having a doctor come to the waiting room to "get" them and call in the parent, then greeting and calling in the child most likely will not only be a surprise, but also will be viewed with curiosity, and welcomed. Curiosity on the part of patients stimulates increased attention, and they can be expected accordingly to listen more carefully and to attend to whatever is going to happen next. I usually continue by asking the child to introduce me to whoever has accompanied him to my office. They usually do so, growing ever more curious about this unusual approach. My expectation, thus communicated, is that they are *competent*, i.e., competent to understand my request and then do it. Because I often know the diagnosis (of "tics" or "habits" or "movements," or even of TS) in advance, I also am aware that they have a problem that makes them feel incompetent and upon which people commonly focus when they meet them, i.e., their facial or other tics, their vocalizations, or both.

Thus *confusion and illogic*, however matter-of-factly portrayed, is used at the very outset to *disrupt maladaptive sets* (however innocuous they unconsciously seemed) and *set the tone for at least the possibility of difference and change* (Zeig, 1985).

As we move from the waiting room to the office I invite the young patient to "lead the way" (rather than my leading the way) as I give directions from behind as to which way to turn. This continuation of "a different kind of place, a different kind of doctor" facilitates the beginning of *shifts*, which are, after all, why the family came to the office in the first place. The metaphor provided (and planted as a seed to be nurtured as we continue) is that each of us can lead the other.

In the office I begin to talk with the young patient directly, taking what is, at least on the surface, a conventional "history of the present problem." Aware of, and focused on, the importance of words and phrases as symbols of the way people think, I begin to consider ways that I might reframe the way the patient talks about his or her "problem" of tics. I usually ask quite directly, "So, why did you come over today?" The response, verbal or nonverbal or both, always teaches me something important about patients, about their ability to understand, about their relationship with their parents, and something about the way they have thought about and articulated about their tics up to this moment. Sometimes the response is to defer to the parent; sometimes it is one of surprise that I would ask him or her the question rather than asking the parent, and sometimes it is a straightforward "...'cause I've got these habits" or "tics" or "twitches," or "I do these funny things sometimes." Sometimes the response is an angry one: "I don't know; why don't you ask *her*. It was *her* idea to come here!" But the purpose has been accomplished: to get the proverbial ball rolling, get the conversation about the tics going, and to do so reasonably quickly, matter-of-factly, and in as unthreatening a way as possible.

Sometimes it appears important to explain why I ask the child rather than the parent, and in turn children are readily accepting of the explanation that since I am a kid's doctor and he is a kid with a problem, I thought I could get the most important and honest information from the one who had the problem. This usually suffices for both child and parent, and begins to embed and cement the expectation that I will be *their* ally—usually without creating a "taking sides" response in the parent.

While taking the history about tics, I take especially careful notes, asking the patient first if it is okay to do so "because I don't want to forget what you tell me." And there is no deception; *I wish to remember the precise language they use* so that I may assiduously avoid that which is negative and reproduce that which is positive, both in and out of the more formal hypnotic work that may follow. Knowing the language in which they operate allows me to match their kind of language, and to shift it as needed when we begin to focus hypnotically more directly. So, as the child talks about the tics, I note what he says and how he says it. After I invite him to "please tell me about those movements you mentioned so I can understand it," I note whether the child says, for example, "Well, they *happen* mostly when I'm tired," as compared to, for example, "Well, I *do* them when I'm tired." Although the patients are usually unaware of this distinction consciously, the fact that tics "happen" to them implies a belief or perception that these tics are external, out of their control, and are wreaking havoc upon their person. "Doing" the tics, in contrast, implies that at some level they know or think that there is personal involvement and that there is perhaps even some awareness of a potential for control, although they are not likely to agree with a direct, conscious statement about this.

I strive to know as much as I can about the chronology of appearance and disappearance of the tics (when they "wax and wane") as well as what has been *done* about them in the past. Thus, from whom has the family sought advice, treatment, counseling, and how did those interventions help or not help? What were they told and what did they *think* of that? (I always make it a point to ascertain the child's perception and opinion *before* the parent's perception, again reinforcing the underlying idea that I believe the child is competent to perceive and articulate opinions, and that I value them.) A clear understanding of the circumstances of recent and current tics is mandatory, including the nature of each motor or vocal tic, the frequency, the response of others, the patient's reaction to the responses (i.e., what does he do or think, or how does he feel, when friends ask about it? when people stare? when people make disparaging remarks? when parents comment?), and what current interventions are being used.

It is vital to know what the patient thinks the *reason* is for the tics or TS and what the parent thinks, as well as to know their understanding of what TS *is*, even if they've known the "official" name or diagnosis for a long time. This information will have important developmental and therapeutic implications. Young children commonly conceptualize illness or behaviors or abnormalities magically and concretely, often as some sort of punishment for wrongdoing; older children may be more likely to understand something about cause and effect and, as they become preteens and teenagers, may have some understanding about at least a temporal relationship between stressful things in their lives and physical/physiological responses thereto. Beyond the crucial developmental considerations, the newly involved clinician must clarify what families have been told and by whom, what model of understanding their primary treating clinician has for TS, and to what degree he or she ascribes to that description and understanding of TS. This information is important for the clinician about to consider hypnotherapy, in order to be able to reinforce what the family knows and believes that is accurate, clarify and or reframe that which is not accurate or confusing, and integrate hypnotic strategies into their existing belief system.

As clarity is established about the history in the first visit, it is important to understand what the patient thinks is the reason for this particular visit to you: how she got this appointment, who referred her, what she thinks is supposed to "happen" here, and so forth. This not only clarifies child and parent expectations and provides an easy starting place for talk about hypnosis if the subject comes up, but also lets the clinician know, for example, about the parent–child relationship, how the child was prepared for the visit today, and similar factors.

Using humor and continuing to offer the message that "you are important and so is your opinion," I often ask the child directly, "Well, what was *I* supposed to do…?" Usually the child or parent knows something, and the response may be as simple as "You're supposed to hypnotize me" (to which I commonly respond by saying, "Oh, what's 'hypnotize'?" or, "Really? I only know how to hypnotize one person, and that's me. All hypnotizing is self-hypnotizing. But if *you* want to *learn* how to hypnotize for *yourself*, like to help with those tics that you were telling me about, then I'm a good coach and I can help you with that…"). Other common child responses are "To learn relaxing and imagining" and "For biofeedback, whatever that is…" And then one can move into a comfortable discussion of what the parents' and child's beliefs and understandings are about hypnosis before mistakenly jumping into a canned speech about what hypnosis is or is not. Once I know what they think or know, then I can provide reinforcement, clarification, or demystification and correction before moving on to setting a plan for subsequent visits.

Prior to the conclusion of a first visit, I wish to *provide positive expectations for positive outcomes*. Accordingly, I ask the parents and child to complete an inventory about tics and ask the youngster to maintain a daily or twice daily log of tic behaviors, giving himself or herself a rating on a 0–12 scale for how much the tics were occurring, and sometimes on a second 0–12 scale for how troublesome they were. Even children who have grown tired of or bored with completing the log can usually be easily motivated to do so by simply explaining, "One way to be really sure that the things I can show you how to do are *helping* is to measure how the tics *are*, and you're the best one to do that *because you know better than anyone how your* *tics are, how they feel...So please do this for yourself...*not forever, but just for *a while* [purposely open-ended suggestion] *until you begin to see the results you want."* (These embedded suggestions and the expectation of seeing the results he wants are offered matter-of-factly.) *Asking the child to do something* in this fashion is designed to increase his focus on the problem behavior (tics), both to disrupt the prior expectations about not paying attention to it, and to have him notice that the tics really are not just "there" or " not there," but, like most behaviors, exist across a spectrum. Continuing to use a matter-of-fact and humor-based approach, I ask the child if he will miss the tics when they're gone. He, of course, says no, but again the embedded suggestion *"when* they're gone" means that there's hope, that there is an expectation that they *will* be gone, without any implied promise as to when, to what extent, or for how long.

I am then clear to explain to the child what will occur next time:

At the next visit it will be you and me meeting privately. Perhaps if you want we can watch a video of another kid learning and doing what I can teach you, and if you want your Mom or Dad can watch that with us. Then we'll look at your calendar and see how you've been doing, so please bring it along; and then we'll get into *learning some things about how to get better control* than you *already* have. [The sentence is phrased to imply that I believe that he already has *some* control.] Okay?

The child's agreement is affirmation that he has been listening and has at least a beginning level of commitment to move forward in this together.

In the context of such a first visit the taking of the history and the development of rapport are integrated naturally with the presentation of ideas in ways that allow the individual to begin to think about using them to stimulate change (within himself) (Zeig, 1985).

Issues in Hypnosis

The first "official" hypnotic experience usually flows naturally and easily after the initial session. Motivated to make a change, most children learn easily and quickly and probably do so because they are closely in tune with and familiar with their unconscious through their imagination. *Induction,* or a formalized and more concrete beginning of hypnosis, *is relatively quick and easy,* particularly because the clinician has already developed at least a beginning and comfortable rapport with the child and knows something about her likes and dislikes. After all, the hypnotic relationship already began at the first visit with positive suggestions and the creation of a context in which suggestions could be accepted for the purpose of helping. On a more concrete level, the parent and child learned at the previous visit that this time the child could expect to "learn hypnosis."

Gardner and Olness (1988) have emphasized the importance of selecting induction strategies and tailoring hypnotic suggestions and language to the specific developmental level and needs of the child. As with anything we do with children, the manner in which we develop rapport, the "induction" strategies, the language utilized, and the content and expectations embodied in the hypnotic suggestions must all be understood in a developmental context. Thus, while a preschool-age child understands and experiences hypnosis as analogous to what they do, sense, and feel when they are "pretending," so by contrast latency-aged children most easily understand hypnosis when it is described, discussed, and experienced as "really the same as 'daydreaming,' only you decide to daydream here so that you can learn to help yourself, in your case to learn how to help yourself with those tics that used to come more often." With an adolescent, of course, one must appeal not only to her developing ego and conscience, but also to her understanding of alternative states of mind, with which she already may have had experience, positive or negative, with or without the use of chemical substances. Thus, it might be most useful to say, "You know, this hypnosis stuff is *just like using your imagination* to concentrate on something you prefer and enjoy rather than focusing on the teacher when she's boring, or on your parents when they are reprimanding you— or like really focusing in on something, like your favorite music."

The induction technique, therefore, with most children is as simple and quick as:

Let's pretend that we're at a very special birthday party. . .

or

So, just go ahead and daydream about being somewhere where you have a lot of fun and no one bugs you or bothers you....It will probably help to be there when you close your eyes, and just daydream that you're really there, because you *are* really there in your mind, aren't you? It's funny and neat how you can be there and here at the same time....Great!

or

Take a few moments now to just clear your mind and imagine that you are out partying with friends; maybe it will be like a replay of some really good time you had recently, or maybe like a rehearsal of

some cool time that's coming up....I don't now....Just notice whatever comes to your mind...and enjoy it....Some people like to do it
by closing their eyes and just being there, some like to do it by imagining a blank screen, either white or black, and then watching their
imagination come onto the screen like a movie beginning....I don't
know which you'll do [The message, of course, is that they *will do
something*...]

[I might also add at this point that] Most kids are happy when
they do this, 'cause they realize that they have done it before, but
didn't know they were doing it...or didn't know that it was self-
hypnosis.

Deepening: Deepening or intensification of the experience is most easily
accomplished through focused attention on the patient's imagery with
emphasis on multisensory suggestions, for example:

Notice who is there with you or maybe you are alone. Notice what
you see there. Notice the weather just the way you like it...and the
more you notice, the more comfortable you get, ...and you can get
very comfortable. Notice the sounds there in your imagination, maybe
the sounds of the weather, or voices, or music, or maybe it's quiet
and you can listen to the quiet. And notice the smells, perhaps of the
air, the place, or maybe of something you're eating. And notice the
taste, and really enjoy it because *you are the boss of it*. [Permissive,
choice-focused options within a context are empowering and remind
patients implicitly that they are in charge of this experience, which
in itself intensifies the trance. It is often effective as a deepening strategy, as an ego-strengthening suggestion, and as a positive, "future-
programming" therapeutic suggestion to *point out to the young patient
that he is "doing it" exactly right*, ...and then to "prove" that to them
by acknowledging the physiological changes that have taken place
since they began "focusing your mind this way." For example, I might
note that] "You probably already noticed [this is intended to be and
commonly is experienced by children as a compliment as well as an
invitation to notice *now* even if they hadn't already] that even though
we didn't mention it you are sitting very still...and that means that
your body and mind are communicating very effectively while you are in
this different state of mind we call imagination or hypnosis. You probably also noticed that you are breathing more slowly now than you
were before, ...and that's really great to feel...because *when the mind
relaxes by daydreaming* this way, *the body listens* and responds by breathing more slowly.

Beyond ratification of the trance behavior and ego-strengthening, these suggestions are designed for and, perhaps even more importantly, function as metaphors for the control (over the tics) that the child is seeking.

Following deepening, I often move into *teaching progressive relaxation* by "noticing" with them that "it's natural for the body to relax as the mind does...and you do that very well...and even though you are already relaxed, it would be nice to discover *how much more relaxation you are able to give yourself when you want it and need it....* (Because the agreed-upon problem has to do with tics—i.e., muscles moving in ways that are undesirable—learning relaxation that one can control may well be pivotal as a metaphor for the child.) With children and teenagers with TS, I have always taught progressive relaxation from the toes upward (Kohen & Botts, 1987), purposely ignoring the common sites of tics—i.e. face, mouth, head, and neck—until the trance has deepened, the patient's comfort and pride have increased, and a growing sense of control is emerging. This paradoxical paying of little or less attention to the site of "the problem" allows for and even invites the patient to dissociate from the problem while paying increased attention to himself and increased attention to the therapist, who, unlike others, pays seemingly little or no attention to "those tics."

Specific Therapeutic Suggestions

During a first trance experience I have several (usually unspoken) goals in mind for the patient: (a) that he has a positive trance experience that occurs naturally and easily, thereby setting the tone for future success and comfort within which to learn; (b) that he experience purposefully developed relaxation (if he wishes to) and positive imagery; (c) that he experience and notice a diminution of tics and vocalizations during the trance as compared to his prehypnosis state; (d) that he learn a self-hypnosis exercise that can be practiced at home; and (e) that he hear stories about (and thus learn strategies for) using self-hypnosis to decrease the frequency of, reduce the intensity of, or stop tic behaviors.

I often provide a transition from intensification through progressive relaxation to the therapeutic suggestions by focusing awareness on the way in which tic behavior has diminished. As the patient experiences intensification of comfort, and progressive relaxation continues, I comment on the diminution of tics that almost universally occurs by this time (commonly within less than 5 minutes):

I'm sure that as you noticed your muscles relaxing so nicely as...you...breathe...out...that's right...that you also noticed how nice and calm the muscles of your face are, and how still your eyelids are that *used to be* so busy moving around a few moments ago....It's really nice the way you *did that*, even though just a few minutes ago you may not have known that you even knew how to do it, but now you know...and *your neck learned too.* [The dissociative suggestion that the neck itself could "learn" paradoxically allows the child at once at a conscious level to be absolved of "responsibility" for both having the tic and not seemingly to be able to control it, and at an unconscious level to be able to teach the neck to "learn" how to relax "when *it* needs to."]

I frequently abruptly shift to telling *stories* in order to simply and easily provide the child or adolescent with a kind of menu of options of ways to *modulate* tics. Perhaps predictably, the best source of material for these stories are one's own patient's experiences, because they are familiar and real and require little or no embellishment. One also can create new stories to fit the patient's own unique background, circumstances, dilemmas, and personal imagery. The "my friend John" technique (Haley, 1973) is especially suited for children and teenagers in this regard, because it is "where they live," that is, it is paradigmatic of "greeting them where they are" (Haley, 1973) and helping them move from that spot in the direction they wish to go. Thus:

1. *Stop Sign Technique*

I knew this kid once who had TS....His was a lot more than yours...and he was a little younger, I think he was nine when we first met [The story of a *younger* child of the *opposite sex* who has been *successful* offers a challenge to the new patient's unconscious, and becomes an embedded and "safe" challenge to the child to do it as well.] Anyway, he said he wouldn't mind if I told other kids about him as long as I didn't mention his name....I thought that was fair, you know, so I agreed. Anyway, he told me that what *he did* to help his tics with his mind exercise was to imagine or just see a STOP SIGN in his mind whenever those tics that he *used to have* [of course, by definition this means they are no longer there or certainly are markedly diminished.] would be there. He said the more he thought about it and used it, the more *his* STOP SIGN helped him. He said it would fill up a whole screen inside his thinking, and sometimes it was the shape and size of a regular STOP SIGN, and other times it would just be the same but would be a different color than the usual RED. He *liked* having it be different colors and sizes 'cause that reminded him it was *his* STOP SIGN and he was the boss of it and boss of when and how to use it to help himself. After he used it for a while every day in his thinking, it helped him so much that he would put it up in his mind *right before a tic was going to happen*...and it would STOP it from happening. [Note the reframing here from the typical scenario of a tic occurring seemingly involuntarily, the patient becoming aware of and acknowledging it, and then doing something to modulate it in some way. The hypnotic suggestion scenario which suggests not only heightened awareness of tic behavior already present, but also, paradoxically, an internal awareness of the "intent" or "expectation" to tic *before* the tic occurs. Although there is no evidence that this "really" happens, "reality" seems to be defined best in this case by the experience that young people report. Most children who hear this in hypnosis repeat it back spontaneously weeks or months later as having been very important to them, and they commonly speak casually of "*using* the STOP SIGN to stop the tics *before they come.*]

Related is the issue of *sensory tics*, patterns of recurrent somatic sensations variously described by patients as feelings of pressure, tickling, warmth, cold, or other abnormal sensation in skin, bones, muscles, and joints. Commonly localized to specific regions such as the face, shoulder, or neck, they result in dysphoric feelings, and patients attempt to relieve the uncomfortable sensation with movements that often are tonic tightening or stretching of muscles. Although relief usually accompanies these movements, that relief is usually short-lived, and the movement is then repeated. Shapiro, Shapiro, Young, and Feinberg (1988) noted that whereas these sensory experiences are seen as involuntary, like the tics of TS, the motor responses to the sensory tics are thought to be more voluntary (Shapiro et al., 1988). The term *sensory tic* reflects both the "involuntary character of the sensation and a hypothesized shared pathophysiology for both motor and phonic tics and sensory symptoms" (Kurlan, Lichter, & Hewitt, 1989).

2. Transferring the Tic

This other kid I knew said sometimes the STOP SIGN worked a lot and sometimes it worked less. When it worked less he figured out that since he was the boss of his body he could *transfer the tic somewhere else* in his body where it wouldn't bother him as much and where no one else would really notice. So, when he had tics that other people would see, like of his mouth or his eyes or his neck, he would practice his imagination and relaxing, and then he would just *send the tics from his face...down* to his neck...*down* into his shoulder and sometimes from there he sent them down into his arm and hand and then touched his hand to his leg to send it the rest of the way, or sometimes he sent them right down the shoulder to the chest...to the belly...and then to the legs...and down the leg until the tics got all the way to one foot,or the other, or both. He told me that then sometimes he'd just transfer the tics into one big toe and other times he'd have to divide the tics into both big toes, and then *they* could just tic all they wanted, and no one would really notice and they hardly even bother....Other times he said that in the few minutes it took for the tics to get down to the toes they got so tired that they were either almost or all the way gone by the time they got there....

3. Variation of Tic Transferring for an Older Child

One time I told that story to an older girl I know and what she decided to do instead of transferring the tic to her big toes was to picture in her mind all of the energy of her tics, and just imagine the energy transferring somewhere else...sometimes to her fingers or toes. Sometimes she pictured the energy like electricity, or like water flowing through a tube. She did it different ways, and it really helped her help herself....

4. Jettison Technique

"A seven-year-old told me he liked to picture what the tics looked like in his mind...and then he'd do something like those other kids, he'd move them gradually down to his shoulder...down his arm...into his wrist...and then into his hand(s)....Then he'd roll them up into a tight fist...and he'd hold his fist(s) as tight as he could and he'd take a deep breath and hold it at the same time....Then he'd let his breath out and he'd imagine throwing those tics away....Sometimes he threw them all the way to Mars or Venus....Other times he threw them in the garbage, and other times he'd picture throwing them *away* to the bottom of a lake.

5. Variation of Storing and Releasing Tics

One teenager told me that he figured out he would help himself by *storing up his tics as long as he needed to* and then kind of *get rid of them all at once in some safe way* where no one would notice or care and it would hardly even bother him. Pretty soon he got so good at it that he could just store up any that were *about to begin*, and *save them to some time later*....So, instead of having tics in class, every day at the end of the morning in school he'd just go into the bathroom in private for about 3 or 4 minutes and *do all the tics there*. After a while he got so good that he could *save them all day* and just do them when he'd get home from school, *someplace where it wouldn't bug his family or no one would notice*. [The matter-of-fact use of the words "just do them" implies a level and kind of control the patient desires but never knew he had, and thus is a potentially powerful, positive embedded suggestion independent of its context.]

6. *Variation for a Younger Child: Twitch Switches*

One thing that is really fun I learned from a five-year-old boy. He really loved to pretend stuff, and he pretended he was so tiny…so so so tiny…so tiny that he would go inside his own body on a trip, an exciting and fun adventure around his body! Sometimes he went in through his nose, or under a fingernail, or through his belly button…and he'd make his way around the body, on a motorcycle on the bones, or on a jet ski through his blood….He had a great time visiting different parts of his body: his stomach and seeing the food he ate getting digested, and his heart and watching all the blood being pumped around, and watching his lungs breathe so nicely and easily…in…and…out. And then he'd make his way *up to that computer center we call the brain*. He just loved to look at all of the wires—you know, those things we call nerves that carry all of our signals and messages—and all of the connections, and all of the lights, and buttons, and switches and dials and stuff. He knew, of course, that there were switches for everything, switches for tickles, switches for sleep, switches for hurt, and *even switches for twitches*. And he'd find the switches for twitches and *turn them down…and then off*. Sometimes the twitch switch was one color, and sometimes another, and sometimes it was a pushing kind of switch and sometimes a flipping kind of switch,…but whenever he'd have one of those twitches—that's what he called *his* tics—then he'd just do his imagining and relaxing and he'd find his twitching switch and then *he'd picture it in his inside thinking* and *turn it down until it was all the way off*….

Having provided young people with a potpourri of therapeutic strategies to use for decreasing tics, I seek to further empower them by offering my real uncertainty of precisely *how* they *will do* this—in the face, of course, of my confidence that they *will* indeed do it. I often say something like:

I don't know which of these ideas you will borrow or use for yourself…maybe the STOP SIGN sometimes or a lot…maybe saving them up for a few hours and getting rid of them all at once for two or three minutes...maybe the idea of transferring the tic to some other part of your body...maybe the switches for the twitches. And *probably*, no matter which of these you like and use, you'll probably also come up with some *new ideas* that your inside mind develops to help yourself with.... Or...maybe you'll just decide to leave all of your tics here in the office; I'll guard them for you and you can have them back if you really miss them or need them for something!

Teaching Self-Hypnosis

In an analogous and matter-of-fact, expectant fashion I always teach self-hypnosis as part of a first hypnotic experience. Before conclusion of the first trance, I specifically focus on reinforcing, positive future-oriented, and ego-strengthening suggestions to anchor the positive hypnotic experience, in the context of methodically but naturally teaching a self-hypnosis exercise. This is done with the full recognition that the child will tell you what he needs, verbally or otherwise. Being a careful listener and observer allows the clinician the opportunity to develop leading and pacing in such a way as to follow Erickson's dictum to "go with the patient" (Haley, 1973). Therefore:

Now that you have learned so much so well, the only other thing that is important for today's learning time is how to finish, and that's as easy as it was to begin. But, before you begin to finish, remind yourself how very proud you can be of how fast and well you learned so much today about helping yourself...and remind yourself that the more you practice what you learned, the better you get. So, *when* you do this at home [this is presented matter-of-factly as a given, and not as something new to learn, thus reinforcing the ease with which it can be considered possible], you'll probably find that it is almost as easy as it was today. [This is both a compliment and an acknowledgment that it will be different at home without the benefit or need of the coach, teacher, therapist.] Begin by sitting somewhere where no one will bother or disturb you—I'll ask your Mom to make sure your brother/sister doesn't bug you at those times—then close your eyes when you're ready or keep them open until they close, and imagine something fun just like you did so quickly today, then relax your body from your toes up to your head, or if you want to start in another part of your body relaxing first that's fine, and then tell yourself what you want to know about using relaxing for those tics that used to bother you more...and then stay comfortable as long as you want to and then *when you finish you'll be done*.... But be sure when you practice, and be sure here that when you come back from where you're imagining, that you bring your good feelings and relaxed feelings with you....

The cue or signal to "finish" is, of course, both the verbal suggestion and the silence which follows.

Following a first such trance experience, it is usually important to "debrief" the youngster about the experience. Lengthy discussions about their interpretation of each suggestion is of no value and can be counterproductive and countertherapeutic. An open-ended inquiry to the effect of, "Well, are you all the way back? Where were you [imagining that you were]? What was it like, what did you do, see, feel?" should be sufficient to elicit whatever is important to the child at that time.

Self-Monitoring ↔ Self-Regulation

Before patients' departure I reinforce the importance of keeping track of tic frequency and intensity on their calendars, and ask that they indicate when they have been "practicing" what they've just learned. Later, this traditional or conventional behavioral modification strategy may be easily integrated into the hypnotic training experience, particularly if the patient has taken an interest in and seems at least in preliminary fashion to be committed to the process of writing down a self-rating once or twice daily. This is, of course, a positive hypnotic suggestion in and of itself. When the child accepts the model and begins to keep track, then by definition if a tic can be "11" or "12," it can be "1" or "0." This fact is later utilized hypnotically as a way of creating change. The ruler, therefore, is not a new concept when it is introduced during the hypnotic state. In fact, I may say to the child:

When we do this relaxation and imagining in a few moments, I'll probably say something to you like asking you to instruct your inner mind to adjust it the way you want it.... What number would you like it on the most? [This kind of sudden question, sudden shift, works to again build the expectation, implication, anticipation that what one wants is *reachable*, and to create anticipation of what the trance experience is going to help patients do for themselves. In a storytelling fashion one might then offer a series of suggestions as to ways in which other kids have "lowered the ruler" (and thereby reduced their tics). Similar use of the "My Friend John" technique will allow a reasonable description, then, of three or four internal methods of hypnotically lowering a tic rating of "11" to a "0" or "1" or "2". This might be through imagination of an elevator going down to a lower level.] One kid I know lowered her tic ruler [i.e., her tics] by imagining she was on an elevator at whatever floor the ruler was on, like a 5 or 7 or 9 or 3 or 6 or whatever. If she was, say, at 8, she'd push the button for 7 and ride down to 7…and then she'd push 6 and watch the light go off at 7 and on at 6…and then she'd push 5—and the tics would be less already—and…then 4…then 3…then 2 until she got all the way to 1 or 0. [Or] This other kid I know didn't like elevators, but he loved those slides that slide down into swimming pools…So he put his ruler in his mind along the side of the slide…and as he'd slide down into the water, the numbers on his ruler would go zooming down, and the tics would go down at the same time….That was really cool!

Biofeedback-assisted Hypnotherapy

Biofeedback-assisted hypnotherapy can be a valuable adjunct for the child or teenager with TS. The first child with TS with whom I worked (Kohen & Botts, 1987) utilized several forms of biofeedback as an integral part of his hypnotic training. The second hypnosis session, conducted on the same day that we met, was videotaped with the patient's and family's permission. At the next session, the following week, he was invited to watch the video privately, and his solitary viewing session was audiotaped. It was later noted that he frequently had vocal tics almost instantaneously after viewing himself having vocal tics on the video; conversely, he was free of vocal tics as he observed the video version of himself to be free of vocal tics. He reported that *viewing himself tic-free and vocalization-free while in the hypnotic state in the videotape* was of the greatest value. In his situation he was highly motivated to develop some manner of control of tics, and that alone served as a great motivator to quickly go into trance and for tics to disappear in that state.

The value of such a video "biofeedback" may be similar for others, given the emotional toll of frequent tic behavior. Videotaping, however, may be seen by the patient as a challenge to him to "perform" successfully. This motivation may then contribute to doing well, which in itself is self-reinforcing and generates ego strengthening. Subsequent viewing of such a video could, at least potentially, serve to further reinforce for the patient what is possible, and may also generate the opportunity for discussion about the patient's views of the video (and, therefore, of himself) in a psychotherapeutic or hypnotherapeutic relationship as needed.

Other forms of biofeedback, such as peripheral temperature biofeedback, or tic-specific or nonspecific electromyograph biofeedback, may be most useful as a metaphor for control. Because it is well recognized that children can voluntarily alter peripheral temperature with the aid of hypnotic states (Gardner & Olness, 1988), such a demonstration of "the way your mind and body can work together" provides a child with TS a not-so-distant metaphor for the control that the child commonly so desperately seeks. Thus, as a child in a first or second hypnotic experience observes a peripheral temperature rise of perhaps 4° or 5° F, the therapist might simply offer the observational suggestion that "Wow, it's really amazing what you can *do*....Without any previous experience you have raised the temperature of your finger *just from* [purposeful paradoxical minimizing] focusing your mind and learning this imagination and relaxation so quickly....It really is *great what the mind can learn to do to help the body make whatever changes are important to make."*

Other Strategies That Work

Because TS is a chronic disorder, commonly "visible" and with immense potential to be socially disabling, and because its manifestations are so vulnerable to stress as an important trigger, children and teenagers may sometimes be "doing great one day and awful the next." This awareness demands that the clinician be mindful not only of the ongoing need for sensitivity and supportive counseling, but also of the need to be flexible and to have new alternatives and ideas available to help young patients who get "stuck." Commonly, these scenarios come to our attention when patients come for a regular appointment or sooner than originally scheduled and report that they have been doing less well. Sometimes they know why and will talk about it right away, and that opportunity in itself is commonly sufficiently therapeutic. Other times the stressor is not immediately accessible consciously and will be identified more easily hypnotically. On other occasions patients will simply note that "it doesn't work anymore" or "like it used to" and perhaps add, " don't know why." Sometimes such statements are defenses for an important stressor in the child's life, but they also may represent simple tiring with a given strategy, or maturation with a developmental shift demanding the teaching of techniques more appropriate for an older child. At such times Ericksonian strategies integrated into therapeutic communication are likely to be particularly effective, again focusing on positive ego strengthening and developmentally specific kinds of suggestions:

You know how a lot of times you notice the tic right before it comes? [It *can* be noticed, *you* notice it—not someone else, and it is empowering.] Now, *slow it down* on that VCR you're watching in your mind...slow motion, and *watch (listen? feel?) how it changes* when you watch it again, *because* you are now in charge of it and you're creating it, and you've lowered the ruler, I don't know how much, but you'll find out...just watch, listen, notice. Sometimes you can do that by noticing one TV screen that shows you how you *used to be*, and another TV with you how you're changing and becoming. Let one finger on your left hand lift up by itself when you see yourself there...don't help your finger...when your mind notices it, it will send a signal to your finger automatically and it will lift, notice...that's right...good....Now, on the other screen watch it come into focus the way you like yourself the most...*and with your controller* lower the volume on the other screen, and then make it dimmer and dimmer...and dimmer...until it goes away...Isn't that nice? So, you can do it that way.

After two or three hypnotherapy sessions, and when I know that the child or teenager has a grasp of self-hypnosis sufficient to allow practice and the experience of success, I may suggest an audiotape be prepared for occasional use as a "booster" at home. This is done simply by recording a regular visit, asking the child's permission in advance, and suggesting clearly:

We'll tape it and if it turns out to be a good session and you want the tape you can have it, and if not, I'll throw it away [Some children are confused as to the value or need for such tapes, and it may be important to explain] You know, it's kind of funny that when you do self-hypnotizing or imagining and relaxing, on one hand it's really relaxing and on the other hand *it sort of takes energy to do it*...so, you know how sometimes you kind of know you should practice but don't feel like it?

Well, that's a time when you might want to put on the tape and listen, it's just different from practicing by yourself...*it's like having the coach at home!* Another time you might use the tape to help you help yourself is when you're getting bored with it, or that inside thinking voice is saying that "nothing helps," or times like that.

Such audiotapes are infinitely more valuable than "generic" relaxation tapes, as they are made specifically and intimately for this child, with references directly to him, his personal ideas and imagery.

At a first session or during a routine follow-up visit, as a way of normalizing or "universalizing" the phenomenon of hypnotic training of muscles to "not tic," I often talk with children about analogous training that they have done with different parts of their bodies over the years without really knowing it or paying attention to it on purpose. Thus, "Isn't it interesting how we automatically teach our muscles what to do without doing it out loud? Like how just now you told your smile muscles what to do but you didn't have to think on purpose, 'Okay, now smile muscles, you smile now....' And it sometimes seems like they do it kind of automatically 'all by themselves,' kind of like how we know how to walk....But we're not robots...our inside brains have to tell the muscles how to do it."

And in ordinary conversation with patients I present useful metaphors, for example, discussing with them the process of having learned to ride a bicycle. I ask if they know how to ride a two-wheel bicycle and they say yes. And I ask what muscles are used to ride a bike. After they've mentioned a few and we've collected a list of seven or eight different muscles, I'll ask how those muscles know what to do to ride a bike. Such a way of talking is somewhat unusual and dissociative, as though the muscles have a mind of their own. (This is, of course, part of the problem with TS: that it *seems* as though the muscles act "on their own.") The child usually knows and answers that the muscles know "because the brain tells them." I agree and compliment them, but also tease a bit and wonder with them how that happens, by asking, "Oh, sure, the brain says out loud: 'Okay, feet, you push the pedals; hands, you hold the handlebars; shoulders, you turn; eyes, you look the way you should; back, you sit up straight.' How long does that take to give those messages—20 minutes?!"

Children find this funny (usually!) and say, "No, just one second," or, as a six-year-old recently told me, "Just in the wink of an eye the messages go all over the body!" They are right, of course. I focus then on the learning part by telling them that back when they were two or three or four years old they didn't know how to ride a bike and they had to learn, and I engage them in conversation about when and how it was that they *learned*. In this discussion they often report that one parent or the other showed them how, helped them, that they fell a few times, and "finally I kept doing it and doing it until I learned." This then allows for me to provide the following conclusion and metaphor: "And now it's probably pretty automatic, you don't have to think about it and *those muscles know exactly what to do the right way without having to think about it out loud...because you taught them by practicing.*" They agree.

As do, I imagine, most clinicians, I strive to conclude each visit with compliments, reinforcement, and positive expectations for the future. Thus, for patients and for clinicians, "I'm glad to know that you know what you need to know, and know what to do and how to help yourself. I'm sure that what you have reviewed and learned today will help even more—especially as you keep practicing."

Patient Outcomes

I have developed a treatment approach directed toward helping children and adolescents to manage the stress of Tourette syndrome that emphasizes incorporation of the self-monitoring and self-management strategies of RMI (self-hypnosis) into an overall comprehensive treatment plan. All patients with TS (35 to date) to whom we have taught RMI strategies report that they have benefited. A few have indicated that they learned "only relaxation" and that otherwise RMI had "no effect" on their TS symptoms. Most, however, have indicated that learning RMI has had a significant positive impact on their lives, reducing the nature and frequency of their tic behavior and helping them develop a more positive sense of self-control. The effect of learning self-hypnotic techniques on symptoms often associated with TS—such as obsessive or compulsive behaviors, attention or concentration difficulties, or learning problems—has not been assessed in our patients or in others to our knowledge.

Summary

As described, our process begins with an individual and personalized focus on development of therapeutic rapport. The clinician then focuses on the paced utilization of the child's reality, her likes and dislikes, and her inner world of imagination as the context and reference for hypnotic focus as well as cognitive mastery. The wide variety of effective hypnotic techniques described share the characteristics of clarifying and expanding a positive expectancy mindset, the developing of metaphors for control through storytelling and dissociation, and creating an overall atmosphere in which change becomes possible and believable. The thoughtful application of this approach has added significantly to the treatment options and to positive outcomes for the young people suffering from TS whom I have had the opportunity to know.

References

American Psychiatric Association. (1994). *Diagnostic and statistical manual of mental disorders* (Fourth Edition). Washington, DC: Author.

Aronoff, F. M., Aronoff, S., & Peck, L. W. (1975). Hypnotherapy in the treatment of bronchial asthma. *Annals of Allergy, 34*, 356.

Azrin, N. H., & Nunn, R. G. (1973). Habit-reversal: A method of eliminating nervous habits and tics. *Behaviour, Research and Therapy, 11*, 619–628.

Azrin, N. H., Nunn, R. G., & Frantz, S. E. (1980). Habit reversal vs. negative practice treatment of nervous tics. *Behavior Therapy, 11*, 169–178.

Bliss, J. (1980). Sensory experiences of Gilles de la Tourette's syndrome. *Archives of General Psychiatry, 37*, 1343–1347.

Bullen, J. G., & Hemsley, D. R. (1984). Sensory experience as a trigger in Gilles de la Tourette's syndrome, TS: A Case Report. *Journal of Behaviour Therapy and Experimental Psychiatry, 14*, 197–201.

Canavan, A. G. M., & Powell, G. E. (1981). The efficacy of several treatments of Gilles de la Tourette's syndrome as assessed in a single case. *Behaviour Research and Therapy, 19*, 549–556.

Clements, R. O. (1972). Gilles de la Tourette's syndrome: An overview of development and treatment of a case, using hypnotherapy, haloperidol, and psychotherapy. *American Journal of Clinical Hypnosis, 14*, 167–172.

Comings, D. E. (1990). *Tourette syndrome and human behavior.* Duarte, California: Hope Press.

Comings, D. E., Comings, B. G., & Knell, E. (1989). Hypothesis: Homozygosity in Tourette syndrome. *American Journal of Medical Genetics, 34*, 413–421.

Eisenberg, L., Ascher, E. A., & Kanner, L. (1959). A clinical study of Gilles de la Tourette's disease (maladie des tics) in children. *American Journal of Psychiatry, 115*, 715–726.

Fernando, S. (1967). Gilles de la Tourette's syndrome: A report on four cases and review of published case reports. *British Journal of Psychiatry, 113*, 607–617.

Finney, J. W., Rapoff, M. A., Hall, C. L., & Christophersen, E. R. (1983). Replication and social validation of habit reversal treatment for tics. *Behavior Therapy, 14*, 116–126.

Friedman, S. (1980). Self-control in the treatment of Gilles de la Tourette's syndrome: A case study with eighteen month followup. *Journal of Consulting Clinical Psychology, 48*, 400–402.

Gardner, G. G. (1976). Childhood, death, and human dignity: Hypnotherapy for David. *International Journal of Clinical and Experimental Hypnosis, 24*, 122–139.

Gardner, G. G., & Olness, K. N. (1988). *Hypnosis and Hypnotherapy with Children* (2nd ed.). New York: Grune & Stratton.

Golden, G. S. (1986). Tourette syndrome: Recent advances. *Pediatric Neurology, 2*, 189–192.

Haerle, T. (Ed.). (1992). *Children with Tourette syndrome: A parents' guide.* Rockville, MD: Woodbine House.

Haley, J. (1973). *Uncommon therapy.* New York: Norton.

King, A. C., & Ollendick, T. H. (1984). Gilles de la Tourette's disorder: A review. *Journal of Clinical Child Psychology, 13*, 2–9.

Kohen, D. P. (1980). Relaxation/mental imagery (self-hypnosis) and pelvic examinations in adolescents. *Journal of Developmental and Behavioral Pediatrics, 1*, 180–186.

Kohen, D. P. (1991). Applications of relaxation and mental imagery (self-hypnosis) for habit problems. *Pediatric Annals, 20* (3), 136–144.

Kohen, D. P., & Botts, P. (1987). Relaxation-imagery (self-hypnosis) in Tourette syndrome: Experience with four children. *American Journal of Clinical Hypnosis, 29* (4), 227–237.

Kohen, D. P., Olness, K. N., Colwell, S. O., & Heimel, A. (1984). The use of relaxation/mental imagery (self-hypnosis) in the management of 505 pediatric behavioral encounters. *Journal of Developmental and Behavioral Pediatrics, 5*, 21–25.

Kurlan, R., Lichter, D., & Hewitt, D. (1989). Sensory tics in Tourette's syndrome. *Neurology, 39*, 731–734.

Lindner, H., & Stevens, H. (1967). Hypnotherapy and psychodynamics in the syndrome of Gilles de la Tourette. *International Journal of Clinical and Experimental Hypnosis, 15,* 151–155.

McKinnon, R. C. (1967). Gilles de la Tourette syndrome: A case showing electroencephalographic changes and response to haloperidol. *Medical Journal of Australia, 2,* 21–22.

Olness, K. N. (1975). The use of self-hypnosis in treatment of childhood nocturnal enuresis. *Clinical Pediatrics, 14,* 273–279.

Olness, K., MacDonald, J., & Uden, D. (1987). Prospective study comparing propanolol, placebo, and hypnosis in the management of juvenile migraine. *Pediatrics, 79,* 593–597.

Polites, J., Kruger, D., & Stevenson, J. (1965). Sequential treatment of a case of Gilles de la Tourette's syndrome. *British Journal of Medical Psychology, 38,* 43–52.

St. James-Roberts, N., & Powell, G. E. (1979). A case study comparing the effects of relaxation and massed practice upon tic frequency. *Behaviour Research and Therapy, 17,* 401–403.

Savicki, V., & Carlin, A. S. (1972). Behavioural treatment of Gilles de la Tourette's syndrome. *International Journal of Child Psychotherapy, 1,* 97–109.

Schneck, J. M. (1960). Gilles de la Tourette's disease. *American Journal of Psychiatry, 117,* 78–82.

Shapiro, A. K., Shapiro, E. S., Young, J. G., & Feinberg, T.E. (1988). Sensory tics. In Feinberg, T. E., Shapiro, A. K., Shapiro, E. S., & Young, J. G. (Eds.), *Gilles de la Tourette Syndrome* (2nd ed., pp. 356–360). New York: Raven Press.

Spithill, A. (1974). Treatment of a monosymptomatic tic by hypnosis: A case study. *American Journal of Clinical Hypnosis, 17,* 88–93.

Tansey, M. A. (1986). A simple and a complex tic (Gilles de la Tourette's syndrome): Their response to EEG sensorimotor rhythm biofeedback training. *International Journal of Psychophysiology, 4,* 91–97.

Thomas, E. J., Abrams, K. S., & Johnson, J. B. (1971). Self-monitoring and reciprocal inhibition in the modification of multiple tics of Gilles de la Tourette's syndrome. *Journal of Behavior Therapy and Experimental Psychiatry, 2,* 159–171.

Tophoff, M. (1973). Massed practice, relaxation, and assertion training in the treatment of Gilles de la Tourette's syndrome. *Journal of Behavior Therapy and Experimental Psychiatry, 4,* 71–73.

Turpin, G. (1983). The behavioural management of the tic disorders: A critical review. In *Advances in Behavior Research and Therapy, 5,* 203–245.

Turpin, G., & Powell, G. (1984). Effects of massed practice and cue-controlled relaxation on the tic frequency in Gilles de la Tourette syndrome. *Behaviour Research and Therapy, 22,* 165–178.

Young, M. H. (1984, November 9). *Hypnosis as a behavioral intervention in pediatric neurology.* Paper presented at the 27th Annual Scientific Meeting of the American Society of Clinical Hypnosis, San Francisco, CA.

Young, M. H. (1989, March 10). *Self-management training in children with tic disorders: Clinical experience with hypnobehavioral treatment.* Paper presented to the 31st Annual Scientific Meeting of the American Society of Clinical Hypnosis, Nashville, TN.

Young, M. H. (1991). Tics. In W.C. Wester & D.J. O'Grady (Eds.), *Clinical hypnosis with children.* New York: Brunner/Mazel.

Young, M. H., & Montano, R. J. (1988). A new hypnobehavioral method for the treatment of children with Tourette's disorder. *American Journal of Clinical Hyp-*

nosis, 31 (2), 97–106.

Zahm, D. N. (1983, November). *A clinical outcome study of hypnosis treatment upon the tics associated with Gilles de la Tourette's syndrome.* Paper presented at the 26th Annual Scientific Meeting of the American Society of Clinical Hypnosis, Dallas, TX.

Zeig, J.K. (1985). *Experiencing Erickson: An introduction to the man and his work.* New York: Brunner/Mazel.